Also by Bill Watterson

CALVIN AND HOBBES
SOMETHING UNDER THE BED IS DROOLING
YUKON HO!
WEIRDOS FROM ANOTHER PLANET
LAZY SUNDAY BOOK
REVENGE OF THE BABY-SAT
THE AUTHORITATIVE CALVIN AND HOBBES
SCIENTIFIC PROGRESS GOES 'BOINK'
ATTACK OF THE DERANGED MUTANT KILLER MONSTER SNOW GOONS
THE INDISPENSABLE CALVIN AND HOBBES
THE DAYS ARE JUST PACKED
HOMICIDAL PSYCHO JUNGLE CAT
THE ESSENTIAL CALVIN AND HOBBES
CALVIN AND HOBBES: THE TENTH ANNIVERSARY
THERE'S TREASURE EVERYWHERE
IT'S A MAGICAL WORLD

Taken from CALVIN AND HOBBES
CALVIN AND HOBBES 2: ONE DAY THE WIND WILL CHANGE
CALVIN AND HOBBES 3: IN THE SHADOW OF THE NIGHT

Calvin and Hobbes

1: THEREBY HANGS A TALE

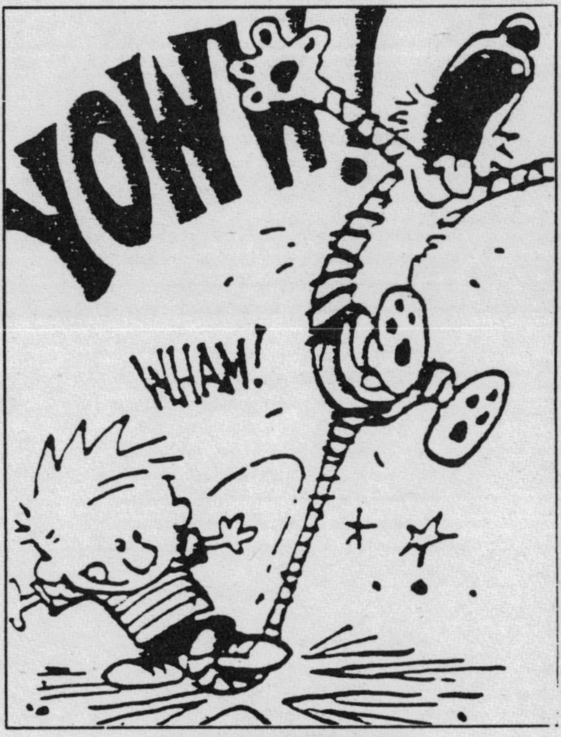
WHAM!

BILL WATTERSON

timewarner paperbacks

A *Time Warner* Paperback

First published in Great Britain in 1992
by Warner Books
Reprinted 1993 (twice), 1994, 1995, 1996, 1999, 2001
Reprinted by Time Warner Paperbacks in 2002

The contents of this edition were first published as part
of *Calvin and Hobbes* © 1987 by Bill Watterson,
published by Sphere Books 1988,
reprinted by Warner Books

ISBN 0 7515 0508 0

Printed in England by Clays Ltd, St Ives plc

Time Warner Paperbacks
An imprint of
Time Warner Books UK
Brettenham House
Lancaster Place
London WC2E 7EN

www.TimeWarnerBooks.co.uk

TO
MELissa

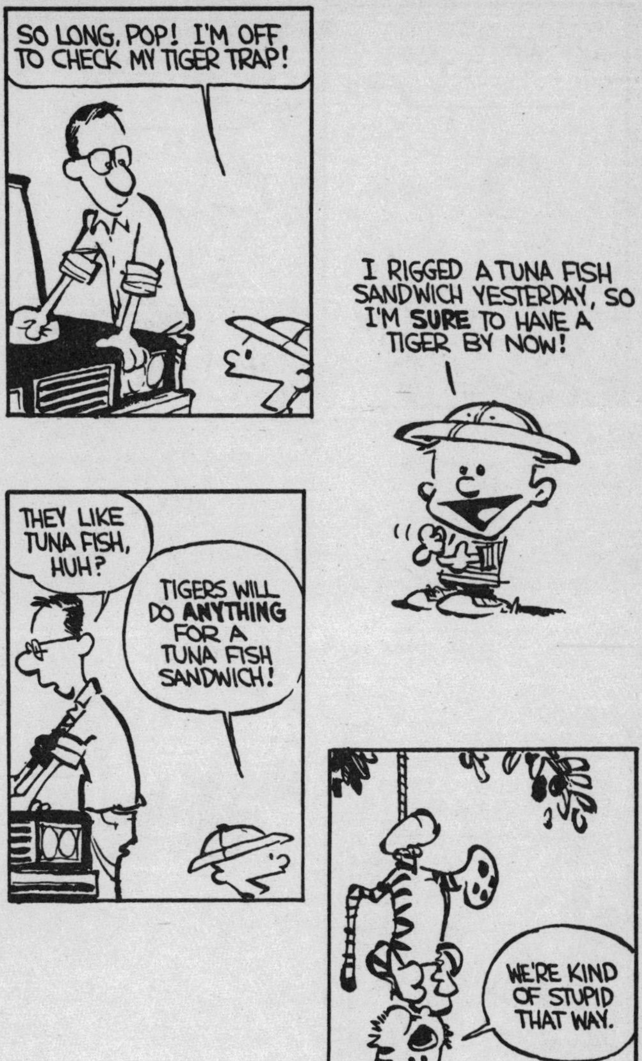
SO LONG, POP! I'M OFF TO CHECK MY TIGER TRAP!
I RIGGED A TUNA FISH SANDWICH YESTERDAY, SO I'M **SURE** TO HAVE A TIGER BY NOW!
THEY LIKE TUNA FISH, HUH?
TIGERS WILL DO **ANYTHING** FOR A TUNA FISH SANDWICH!
WE'RE KIND OF STUPID THAT WAY.
MUNCH MUNCH
WATERSON

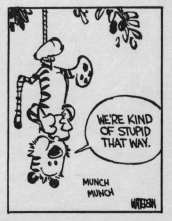

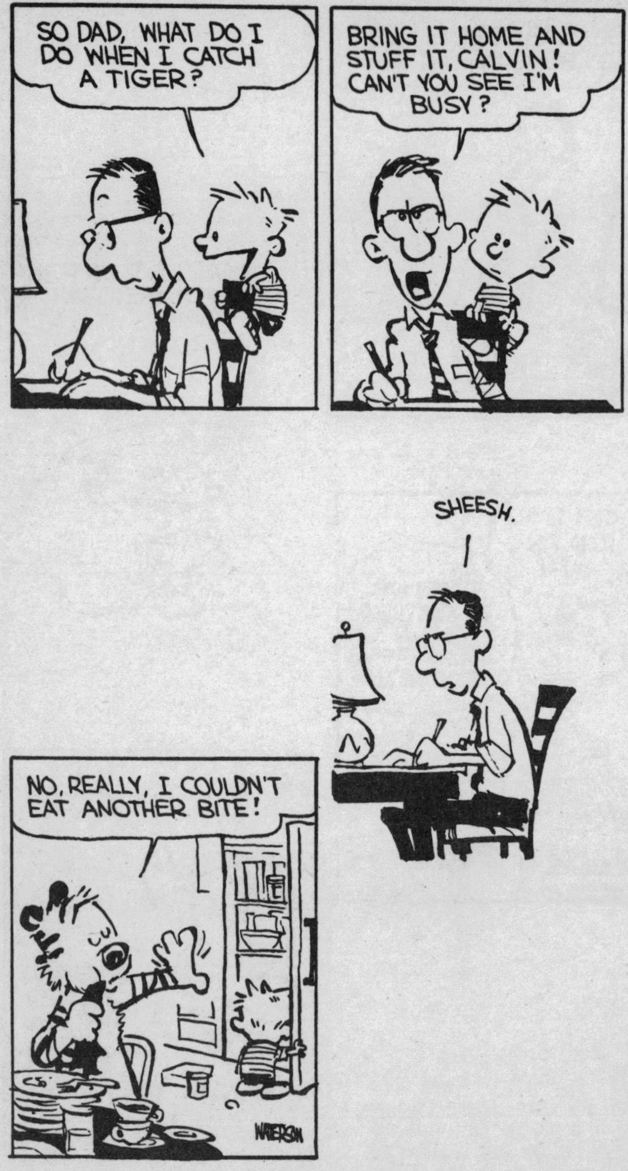
SO DAD, WHAT DO I DO WHEN I CATCH A TIGER?
BRING IT HOME AND STUFF IT, CALVIN! CAN'T YOU SEE I'M BUSY?
SHEESH.
NO, REALLY, I COULDN'T EAT ANOTHER BITE!
WATERSON

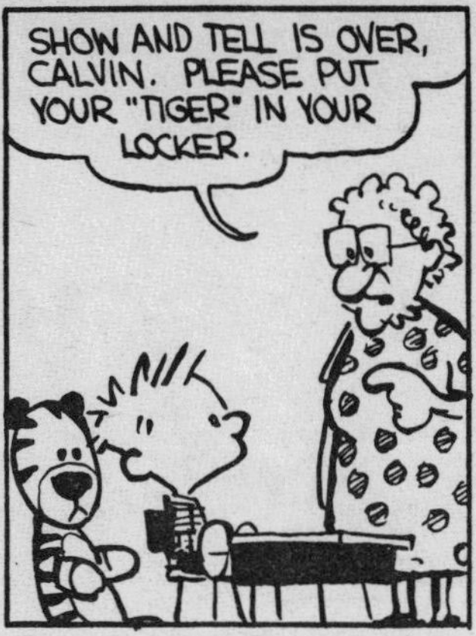
SHOW AND TELL IS OVER, CALVIN. PLEASE PUT YOUR "TIGER" IN YOUR LOCKER.

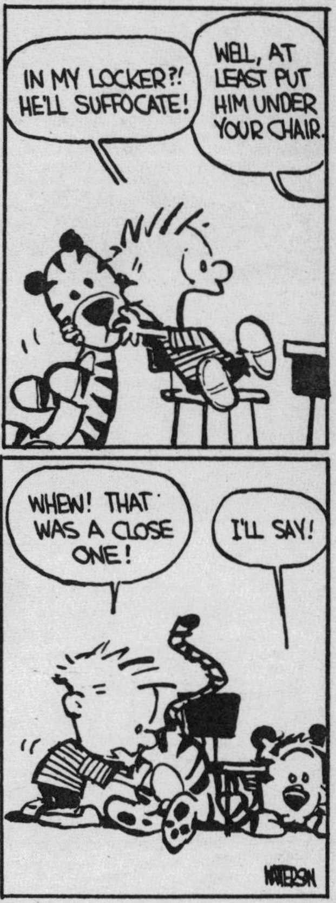
IN MY LOCKER?! HE'LL SUFFOCATE!
WELL, AT LEAST PUT HIM UNDER YOUR CHAIR.
WHEW! THAT WAS A CLOSE ONE!
I'LL SAY!

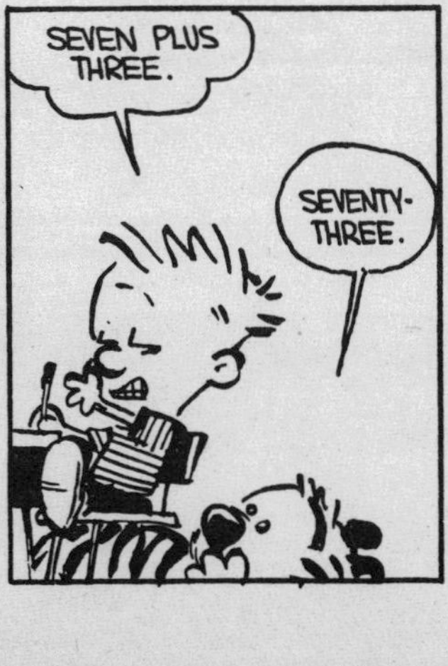
SEVEN PLUS THREE.
SEVENTY-THREE.

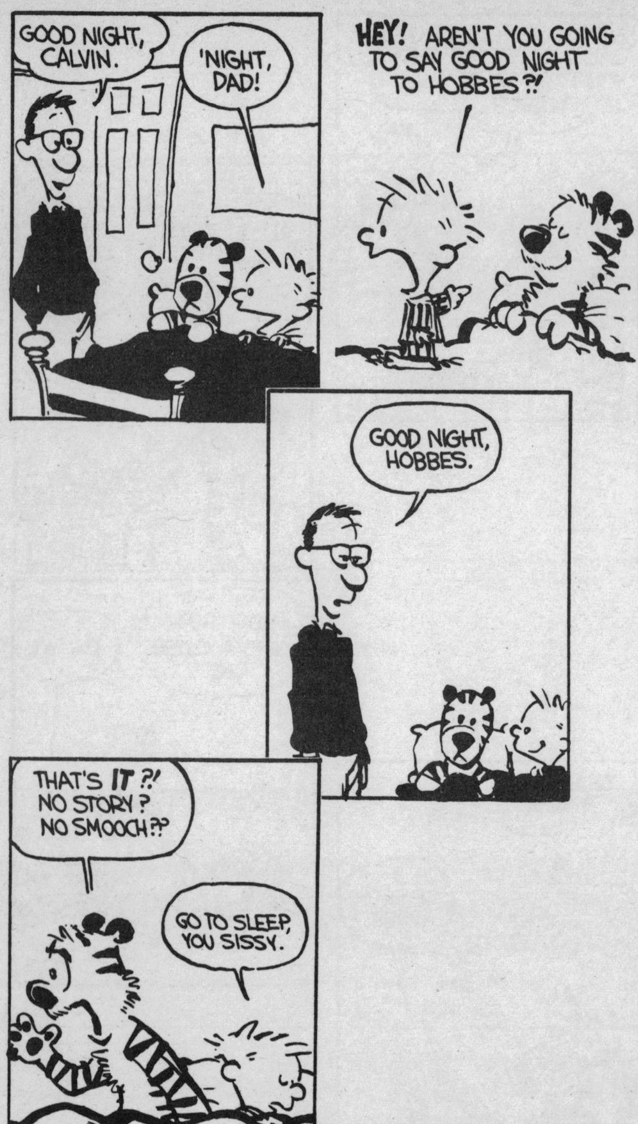
GOOD NIGHT, CALVIN.
'NIGHT, DAD!
HEY! AREN'T YOU GOING TO SAY GOOD NIGHT TO HOBBES?!
GOOD NIGHT, HOBBES.
THAT'S IT?! NO STORY? NO SMOOCH??
GO TO SLEEP, YOU SISSY.
WATTERSON

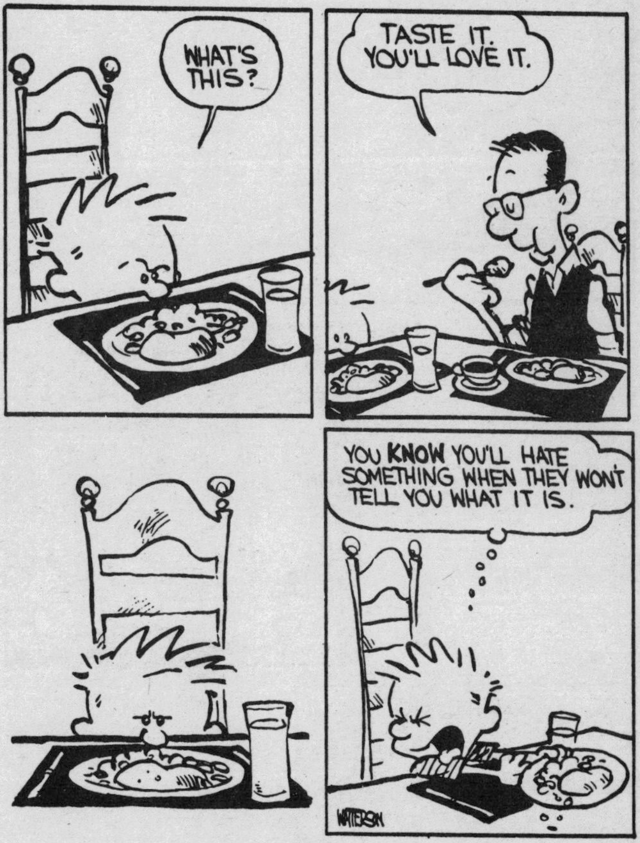
WHAT'S THIS?
TASTE IT. YOU'LL LOVE IT.
YOU KNOW YOU'LL HATE SOMETHING WHEN THEY WON'T TELL YOU WHAT IT IS.
WATTERSON

OUTRAGE! WHY SHOULD I GO TO BED? I'M NOT TIRED!

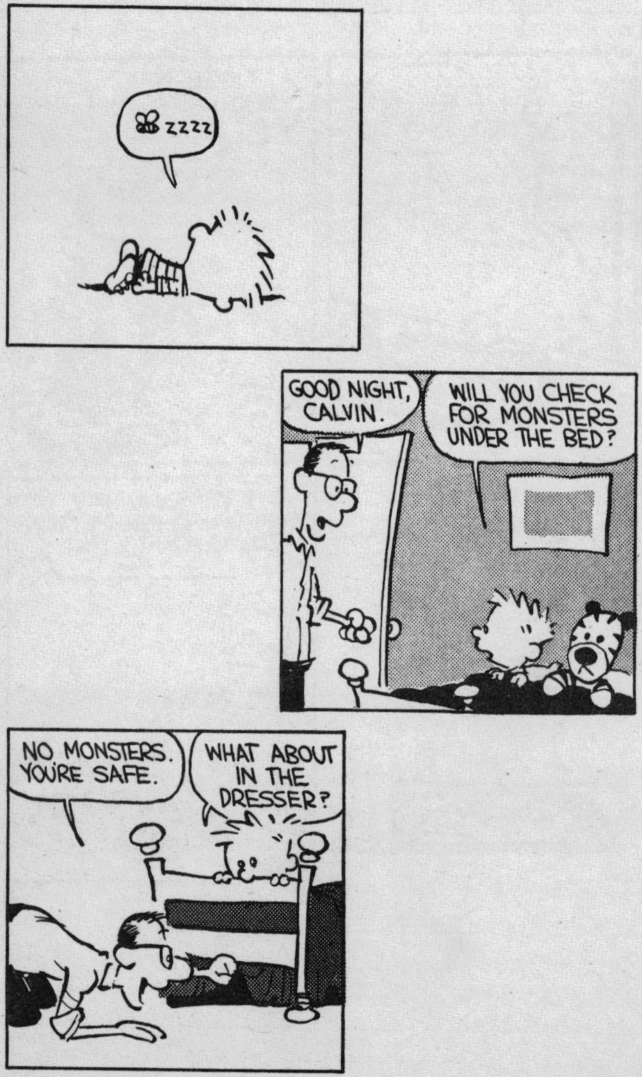
ZZZZ
GOOD NIGHT, CALVIN.
WILL YOU CHECK FOR MONSTERS UNDER THE BED?
NO MONSTERS. YOU'RE SAFE.
WHAT ABOUT IN THE DRESSER?

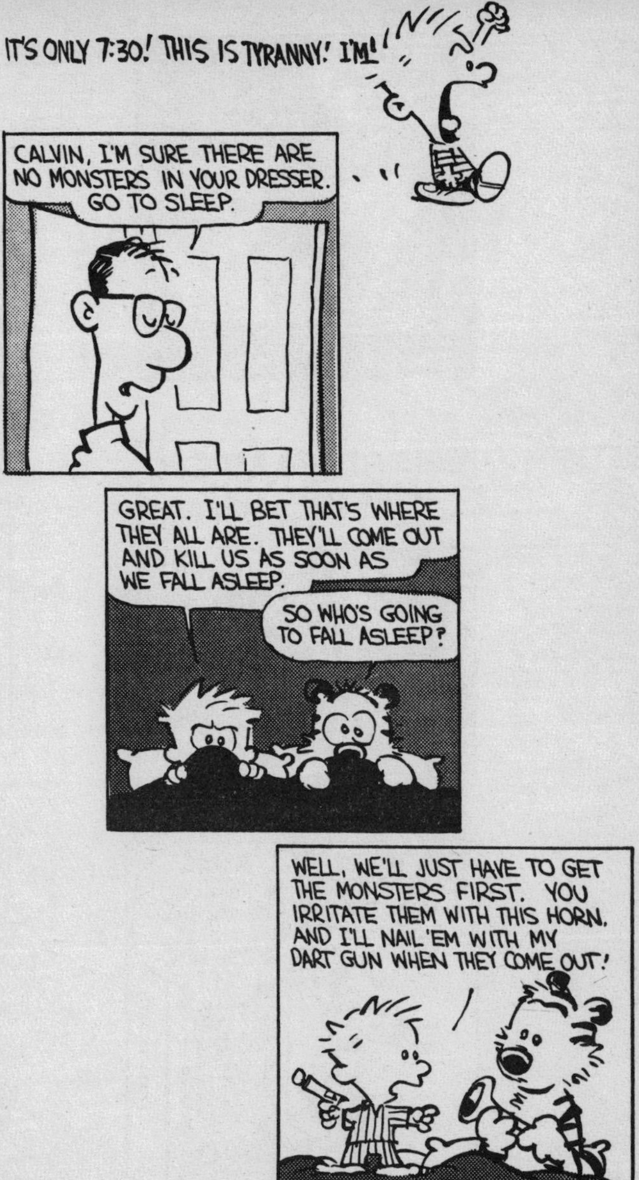
IT'S ONLY 7:30! THIS IS TYRANNY! I'M!
CALVIN, I'M SURE THERE ARE NO MONSTERS IN YOUR DRESSER. GO TO SLEEP.
GREAT. I'LL BET THAT'S WHERE THEY ALL ARE. THEY'LL COME OUT AND KILL US AS SOON AS WE FALL ASLEEP.
SO WHO'S GOING TO FALL ASLEEP?
WELL, WE'LL JUST HAVE TO GET THE MONSTERS FIRST. YOU IRRITATE THEM WITH THIS HORN, AND I'LL NAIL 'EM WITH MY DART GUN WHEN THEY COME OUT!

GET READY! I HEAR ONE COMING!
HONK HONK HONK HONK HONK HONK HONK
WHAT'S ALL THE NOISE?!
AAIEEE!! A MONSTER IN THE HALLWAY!!
DEAR, WILL YOU COME UP HERE A MINUTE?
I THINK I WOUNDED HIM. GIVE ME THE BAT AND I'LL FINISH HIM OFF!
WATTERSON

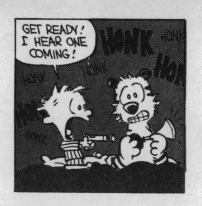

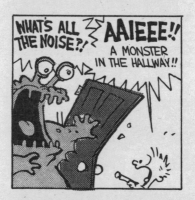

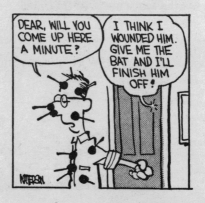

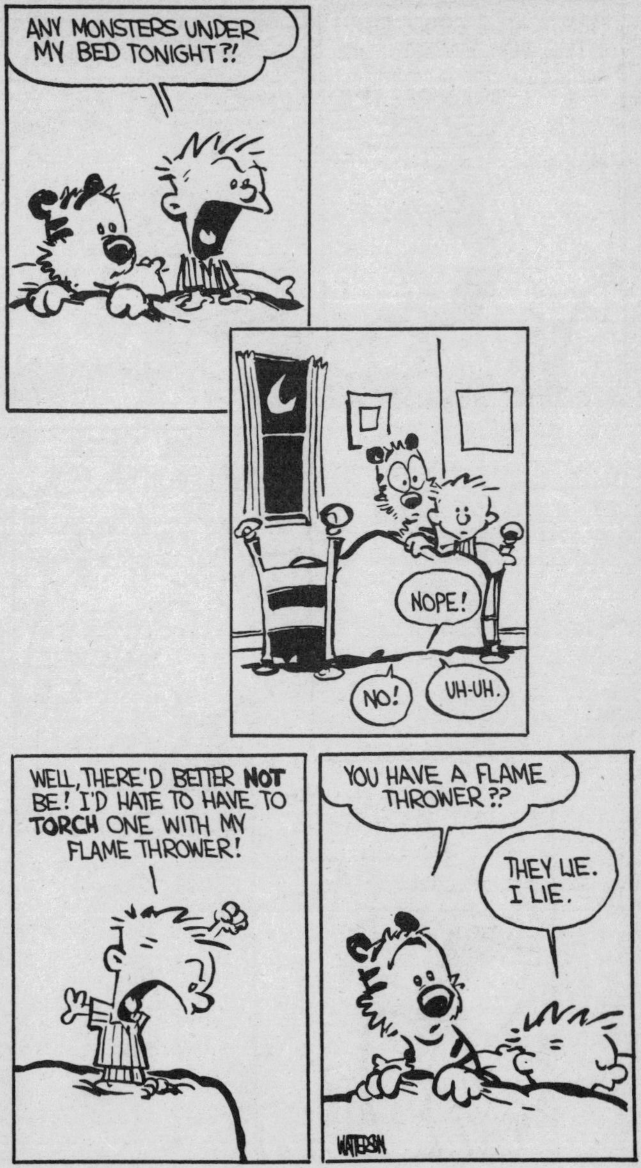
ANY MONSTERS UNDER MY BED TONIGHT?!
NOPE!
NO!
UH-UH.
WELL, THERE'D BETTER NOT BE! I'D HATE TO HAVE TO TORCH ONE WITH MY FLAME THROWER!
YOU HAVE A FLAME THROWER??
THEY LIE. I LIE.
WATERSON

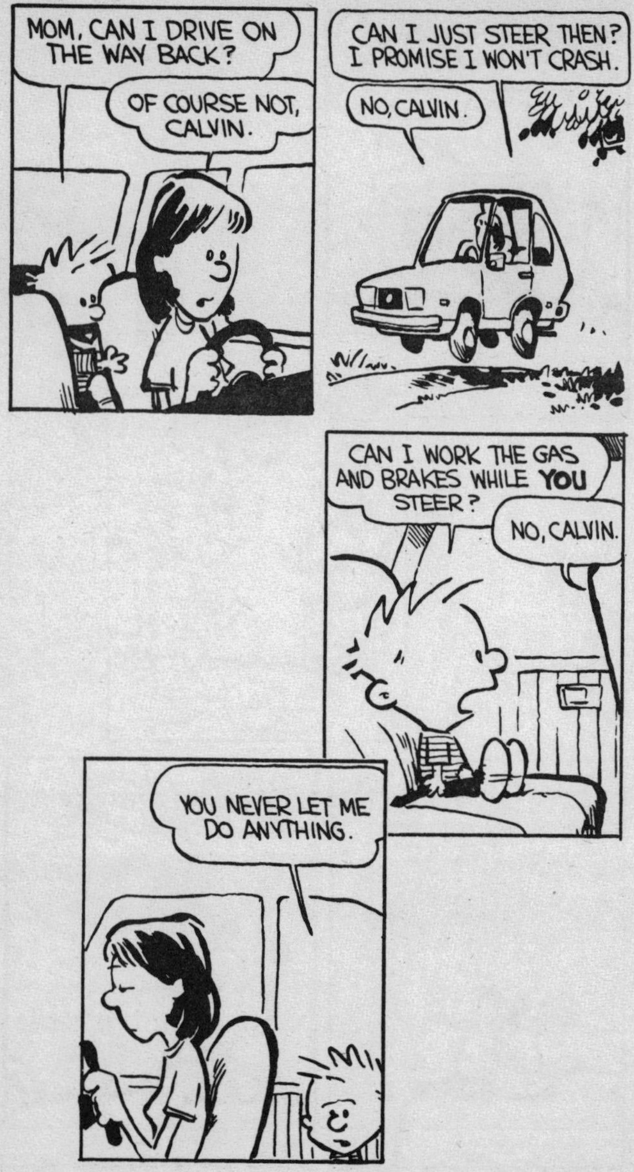
MOM, CAN I DRIVE ON THE WAY BACK?
OF COURSE NOT, CALVIN.
CAN I JUST STEER THEN? I PROMISE I WON'T CRASH.
NO, CALVIN.
CAN I WORK THE GAS AND BRAKES WHILE **YOU** STEER?
NO, CALVIN.
YOU NEVER LET ME DO ANYTHING.

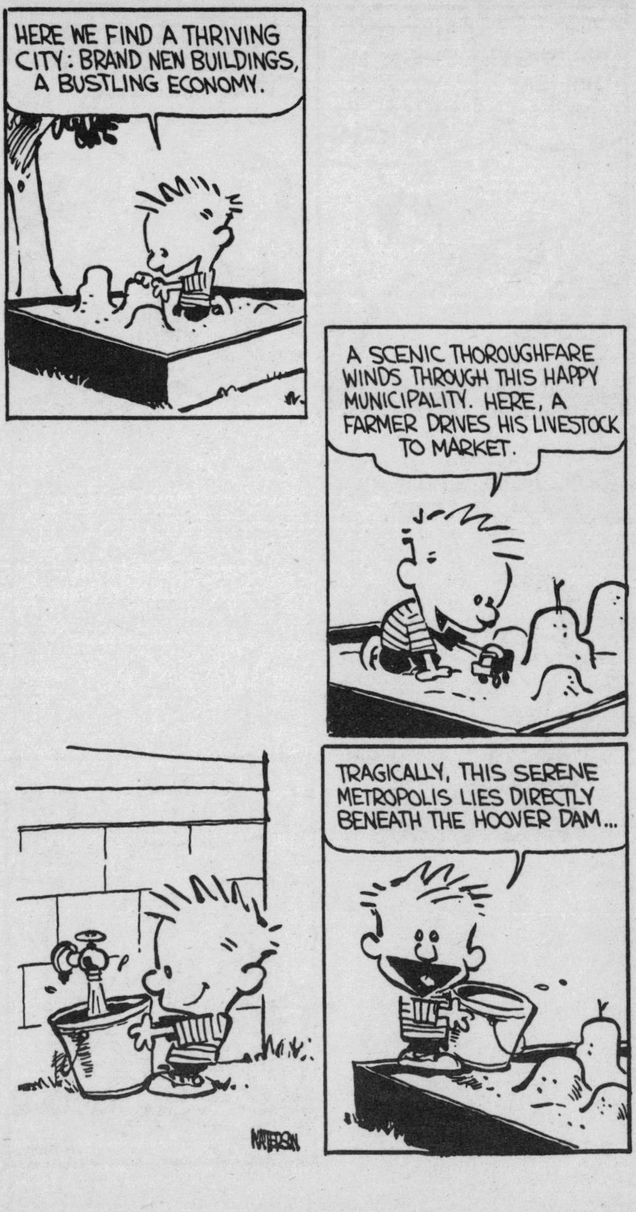
HERE WE FIND A THRIVING CITY: BRAND NEW BUILDINGS, A BUSTLING ECONOMY.
A SCENIC THOROUGHFARE WINDS THROUGH THIS HAPPY MUNICIPALITY. HERE, A FARMER DRIVES HIS LIVESTOCK TO MARKET.
TRAGICALLY, THIS SERENE METROPOLIS LIES DIRECTLY BENEATH THE HOOVER DAM...
WATTERSON

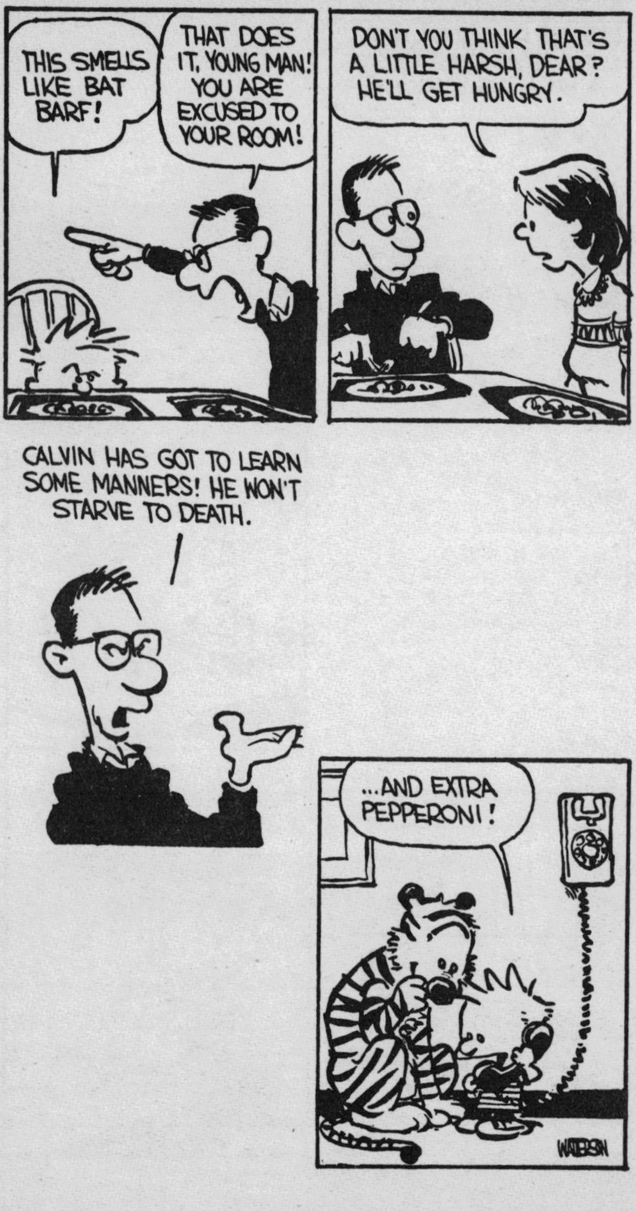
THIS SMELLS LIKE BAT BARF!
THAT DOES IT, YOUNG MAN! YOU ARE EXCUSED TO YOUR ROOM!
DON'T YOU THINK THAT'S A LITTLE HARSH, DEAR? HE'LL GET HUNGRY.
CALVIN HAS GOT TO LEARN SOME MANNERS! HE WON'T STARVE TO DEATH.
...AND EXTRA PEPPERONI!
WATTERSON

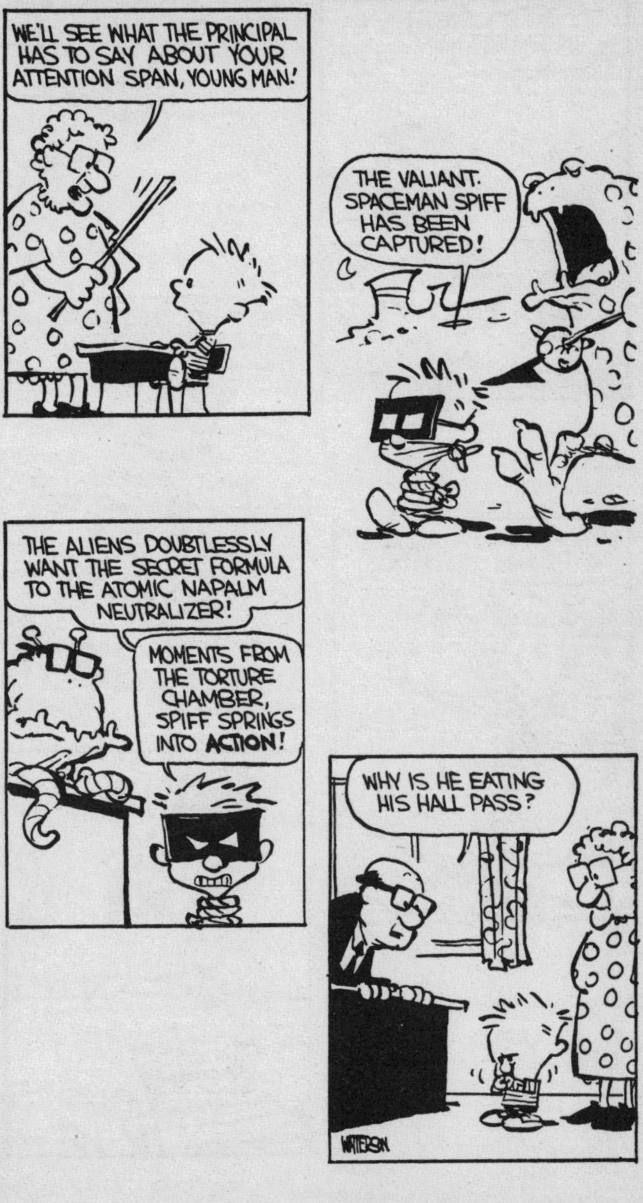
WE'LL SEE WHAT THE PRINCIPAL HAS TO SAY ABOUT YOUR ATTENTION SPAN, YOUNG MAN!
THE VALIANT SPACEMAN SPIFF HAS BEEN CAPTURED!
THE ALIENS DOUBTLESSLY WANT THE SECRET FORMULA TO THE ATOMIC NAPALM NEUTRALIZER!
MOMENTS FROM THE TORTURE CHAMBER, SPIFF SPRINGS INTO **ACTION**!
WHY IS HE EATING HIS HALL PASS?
WATTERSON

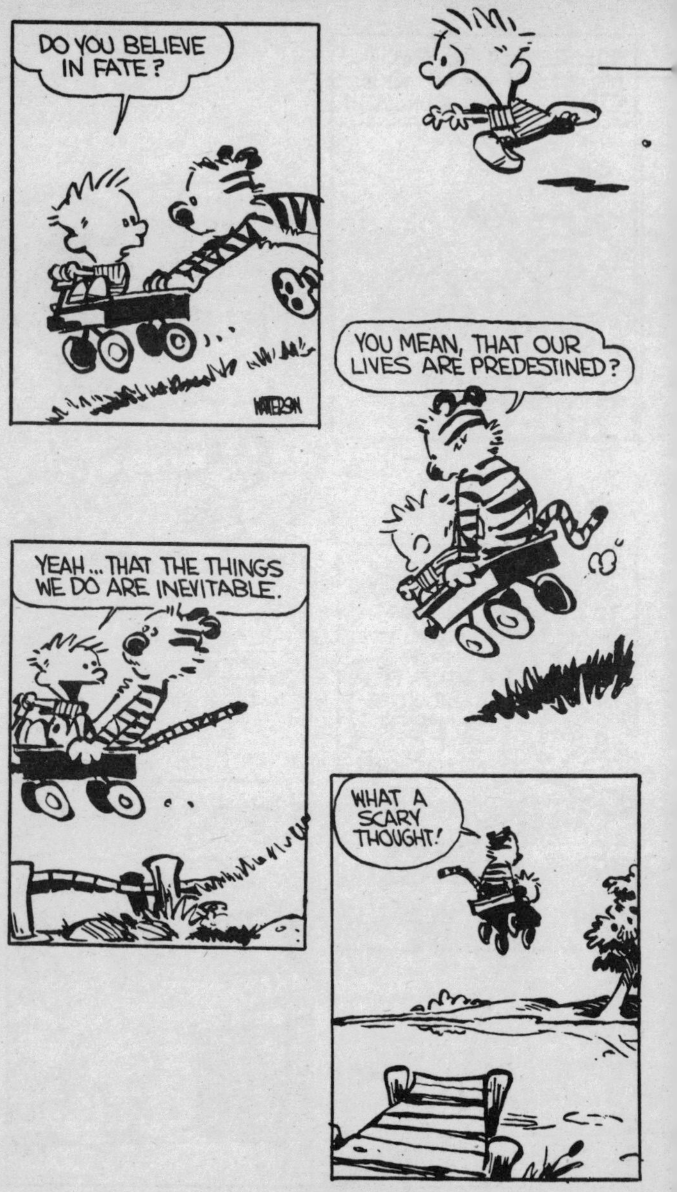
DO YOU BELIEVE IN FATE?
YOU MEAN, THAT OUR LIVES ARE PREDESTINED?
YEAH... THAT THE THINGS WE DO ARE INEVITABLE.
WHAT A SCARY THOUGHT!

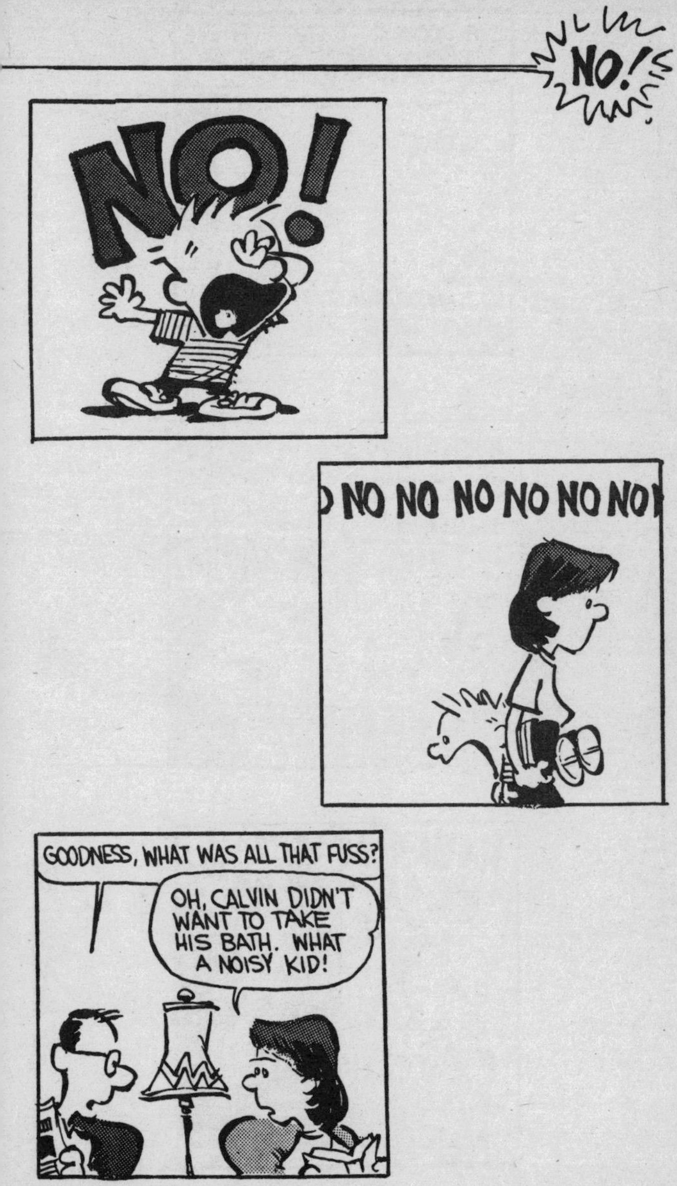
NO!
NO!
NO NO NO NO NO NO
GOODNESS, WHAT WAS ALL THAT FUSS?
OH, CALVIN DIDN'T WANT TO TAKE HIS BATH. WHAT A NOISY KID!

I'M DOOMED. I CAN'T BELIEVE MY OWN PARENTS WOULD DO THIS TO ME!
AH-HA! I'VE GOT YOU NOW, KID!
AAUGH! HELP! QUICK! MOMMM!
HA HA HA! HAVE A DRINK!
HELLP! GURGLE BLUB

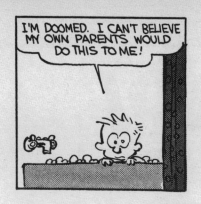

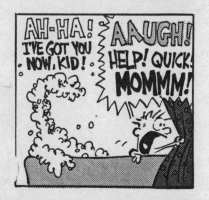

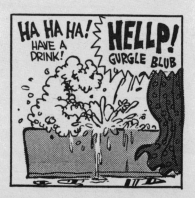

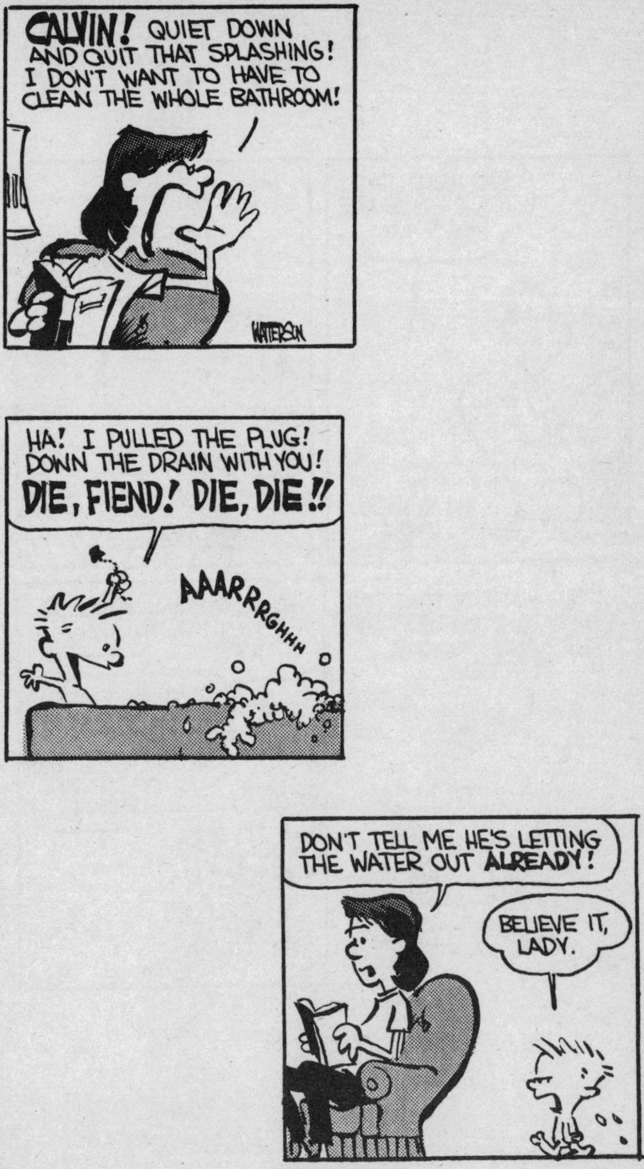
CALVIN! QUIET DOWN AND QUIT THAT SPLASHING! I DON'T WANT TO HAVE TO CLEAN THE WHOLE BATHROOM!
WATTERSON
HA! I PULLED THE PLUG! DOWN THE DRAIN WITH YOU! DIE, FIEND! DIE, DIE!!
AAARRRGHHH
DON'T TELL ME HE'S LETTING THE WATER OUT ALREADY!
BELIEVE IT, LADY.

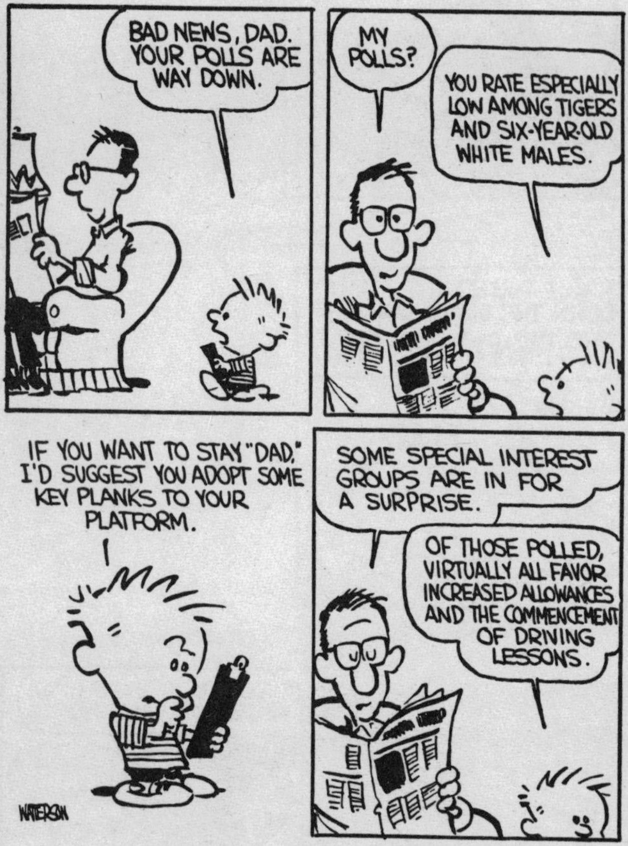
BAD NEWS, DAD. YOUR POLLS ARE WAY DOWN.
MY POLLS?
YOU RATE ESPECIALLY LOW AMONG TIGERS AND SIX-YEAR-OLD WHITE MALES.
IF YOU WANT TO STAY "DAD," I'D SUGGEST YOU ADOPT SOME KEY PLANKS TO YOUR PLATFORM.
SOME SPECIAL INTEREST GROUPS ARE IN FOR A SURPRISE.
OF THOSE POLLED, VIRTUALLY ALL FAVOR INCREASED ALLOWANCES AND THE COMMENCEMENT OF DRIVING LESSONS.
WATERSON

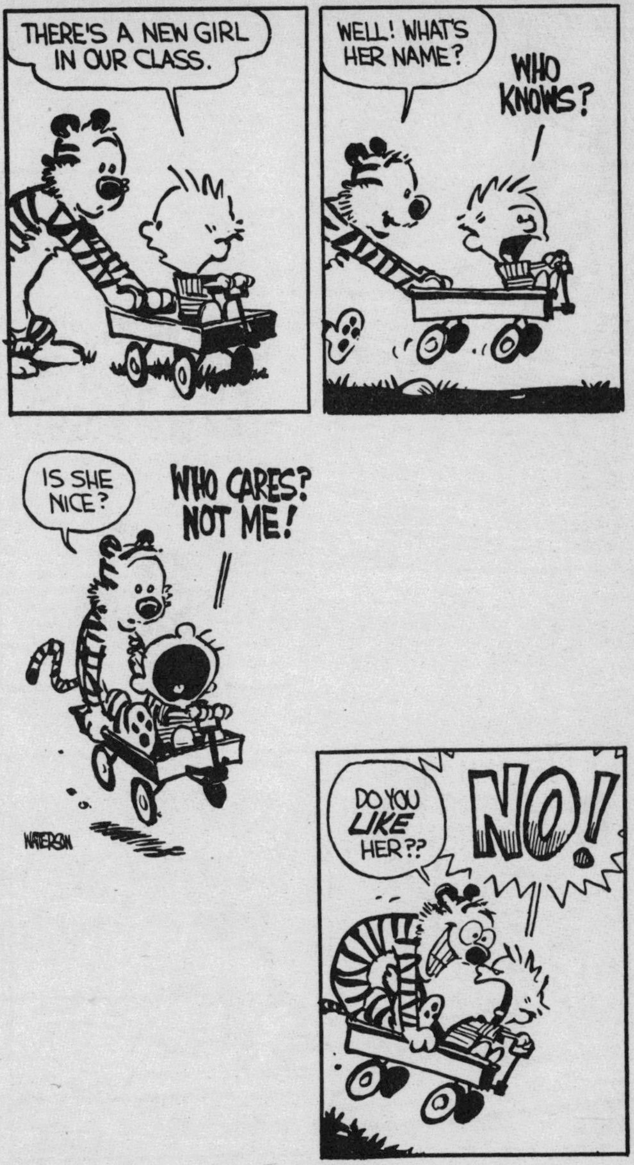
THERE'S A NEW GIRL IN OUR CLASS.
WELL! WHAT'S HER NAME?
WHO KNOWS?
IS SHE NICE?
WHO CARES? NOT ME!
DO YOU LIKE HER??
NO!

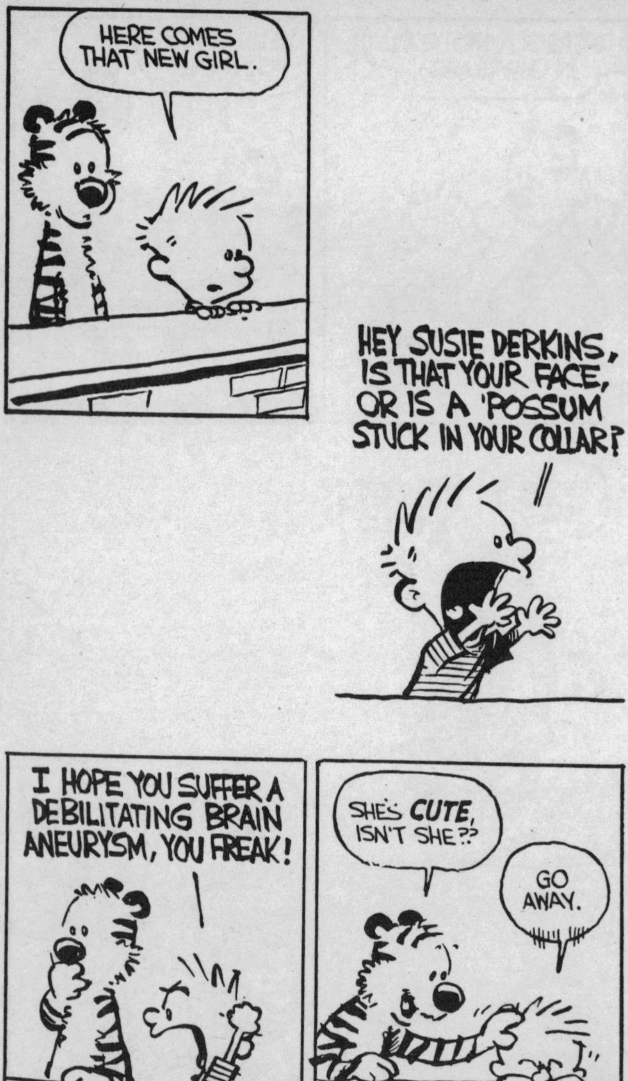
HERE COMES THAT NEW GIRL.
HEY SUSIE DERKINS, IS THAT YOUR FACE, OR IS A 'POSSUM STUCK IN YOUR COLLAR?
I HOPE YOU SUFFER A DEBILITATING BRAIN ANEURYSM, YOU FREAK!
WATERSON
SHE'S **CUTE**, ISN'T SHE??
GO AWAY.

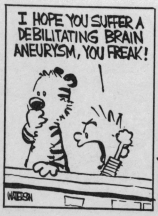

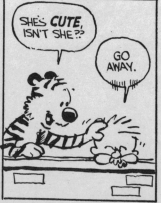

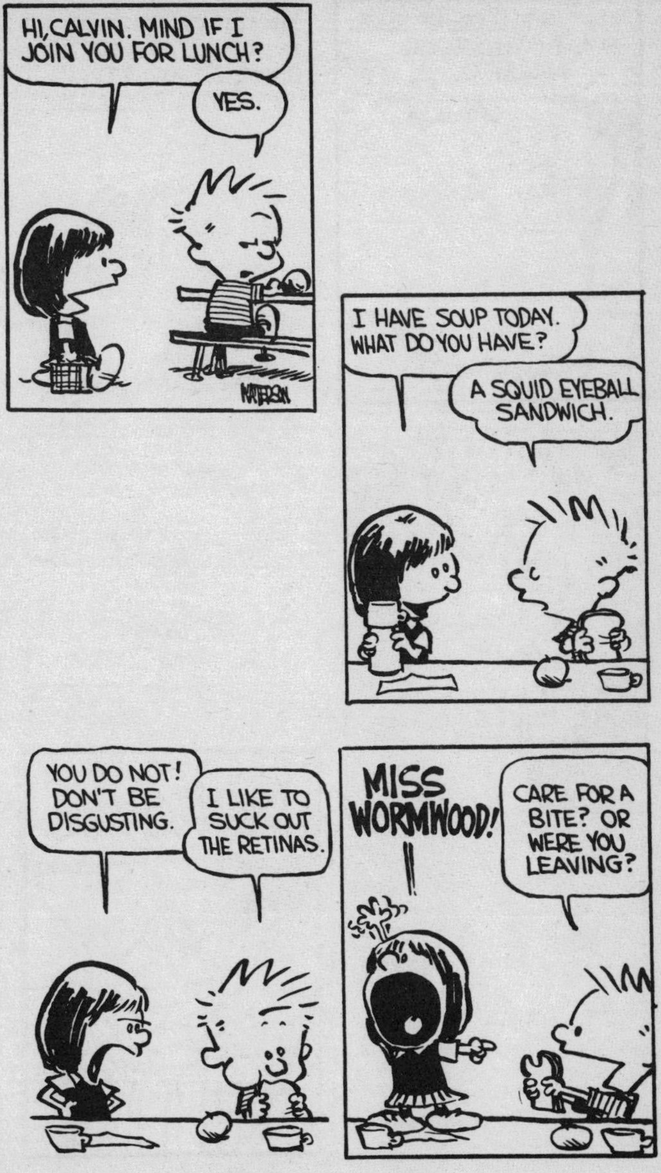
HI, CALVIN. MIND IF I JOIN YOU FOR LUNCH?
YES.
WATERSON
I HAVE SOUP TODAY. WHAT DO YOU HAVE?
A SQUID EYEBALL SANDWICH.
YOU DO NOT! DON'T BE DISGUSTING.
I LIKE TO SUCK OUT THE RETINAS.
MISS WORMWOOD!
CARE FOR A BITE? OR WERE YOU LEAVING?

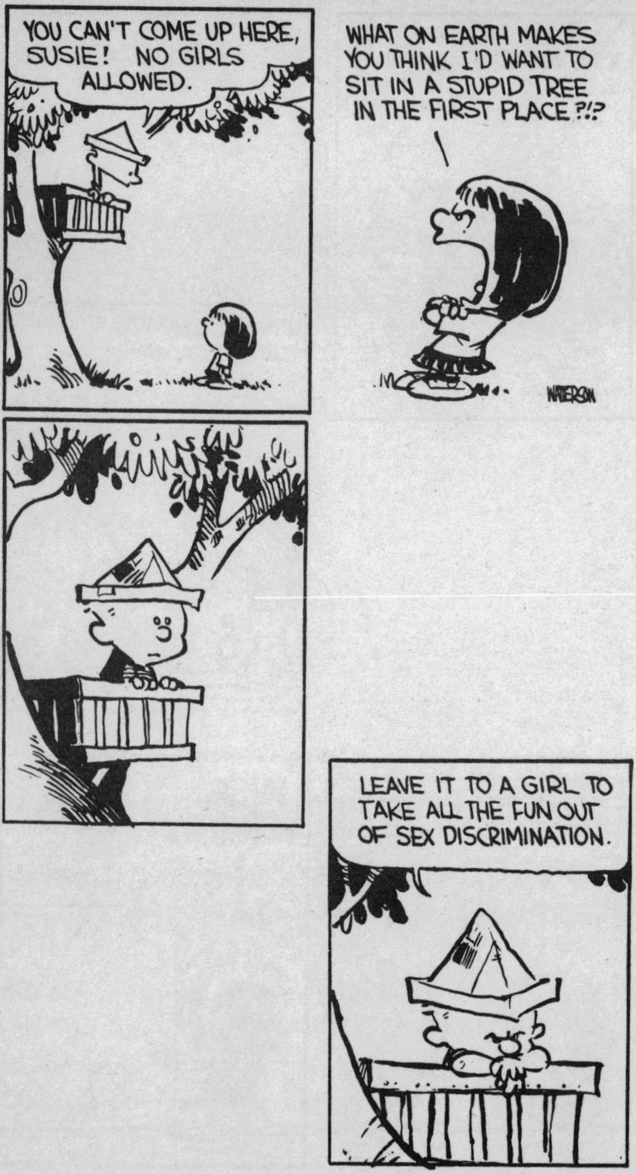
YOU CAN'T COME UP HERE, SUSIE! NO GIRLS ALLOWED.
WHAT ON EARTH MAKES YOU THINK I'D WANT TO SIT IN A STUPID TREE IN THE FIRST PLACE?!?
LEAVE IT TO A GIRL TO TAKE ALL THE FUN OUT OF SEX DISCRIMINATION.

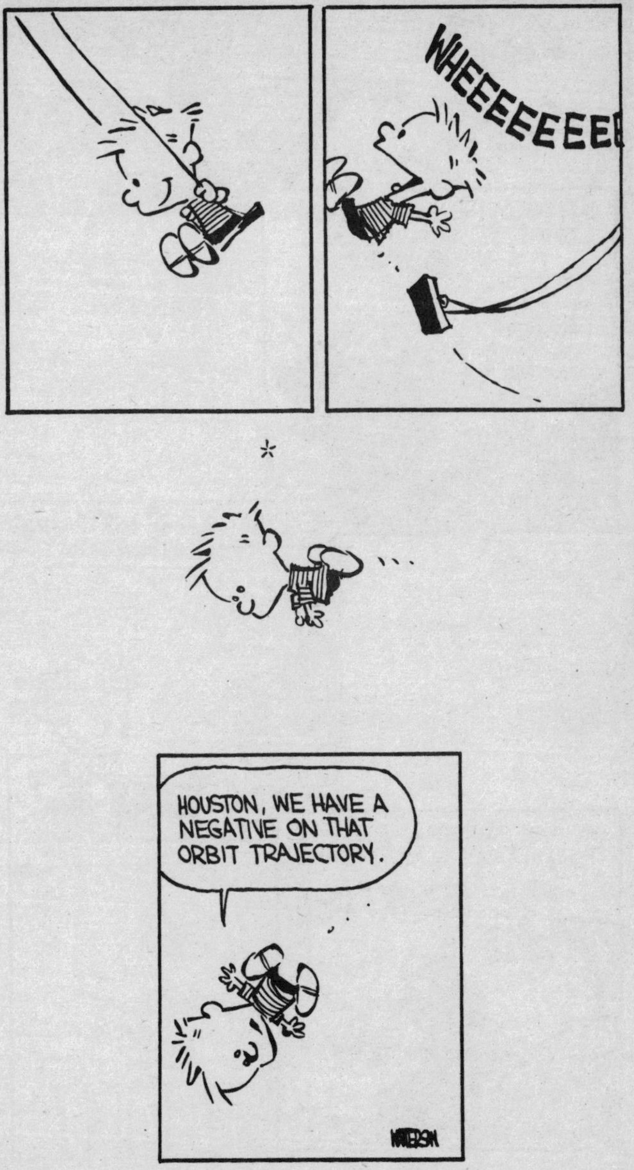
WHEEEEEEEE
HOUSTON, WE HAVE A NEGATIVE ON THAT ORBIT TRAJECTORY.

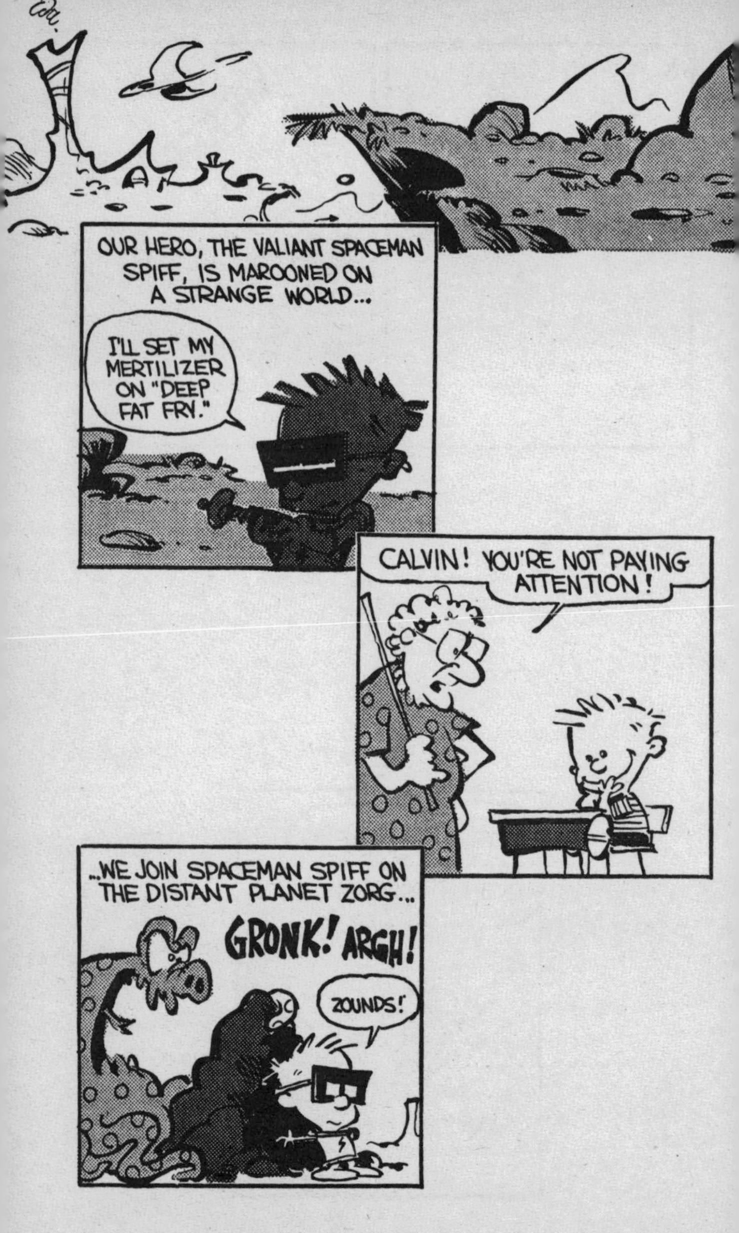
OUR HERO, THE VALIANT SPACEMAN SPIFF, IS MAROONED ON A STRANGE WORLD...
I'LL SET MY MERTILIZER ON "DEEP FAT FRY."
CALVIN! YOU'RE NOT PAYING ATTENTION!
...WE JOIN SPACEMAN SPIFF ON THE DISTANT PLANET ZORG...
GRONK! ARGH!
ZOUNDS!

TRAPPED BY A HIDEOUS GRAKNIL, SPIFF DRAWS HIS TRUSTY ATOMIC NAPALM NEUTRALIZER!
CHEW ELECTRIC DEATH, SNARLING CUR!
BUT THE WEAPON IS USELESS! SPIFF IS DOOMED!!
OUR HERO MAKES A BREAK, AND DUCKS INTO A NEARBY CAVE!

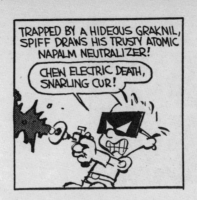

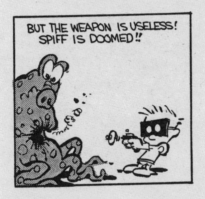

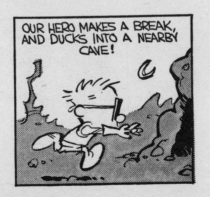

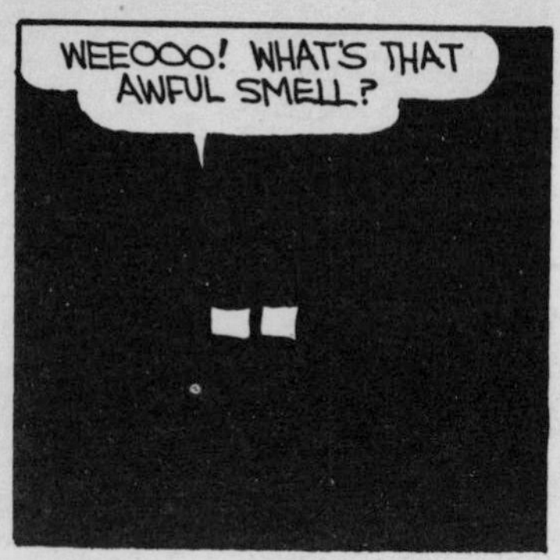
WEEOOO! WHAT'S THAT AWFUL SMELL?

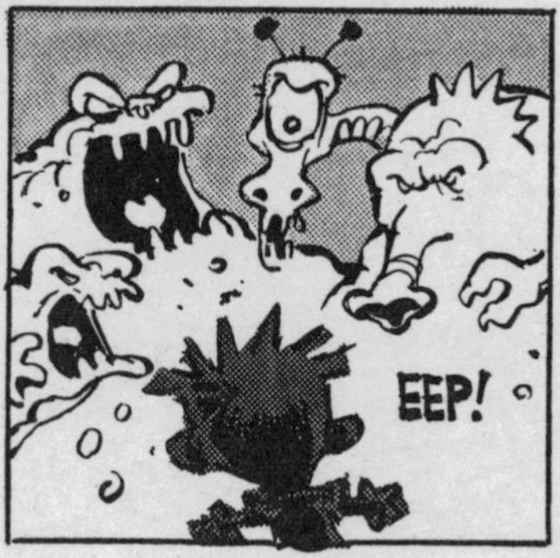
EEP!

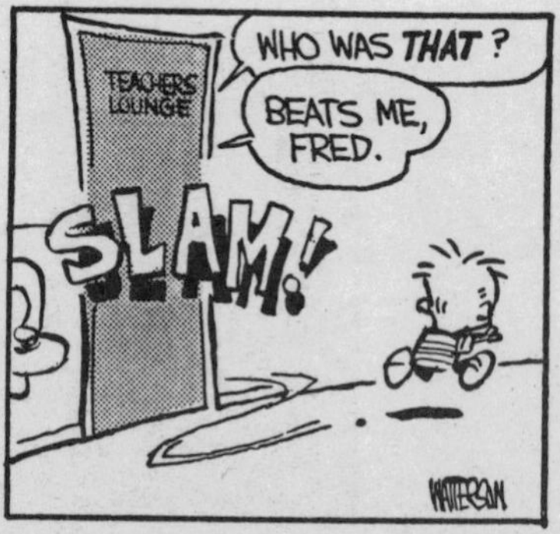
TEACHERS' LOUNGE
WHO WAS *THAT* ?
BEATS ME, FRED.
SLAM!
WATTERSON

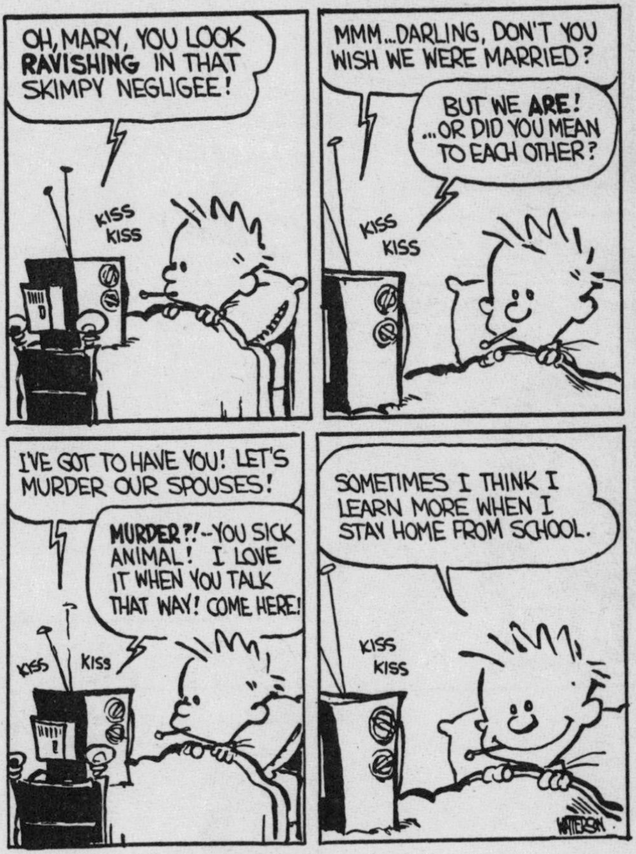
OH, MARY, YOU LOOK **RAVISHING** IN THAT SKIMPY NEGLIGEE!
KISS KISS
MMM...DARLING, DON'T YOU WISH WE WERE MARRIED?
BUT WE **ARE**! ...OR DID YOU MEAN TO EACH OTHER?
KISS KISS
I'VE GOT TO HAVE YOU! LET'S MURDER OUR SPOUSES!
MURDER?!--YOU SICK ANIMAL! I LOVE IT WHEN YOU TALK THAT WAY! COME HERE!
KISS KISS
SOMETIMES I THINK I LEARN MORE WHEN I STAY HOME FROM SCHOOL.
KISS KISS
WATERSON

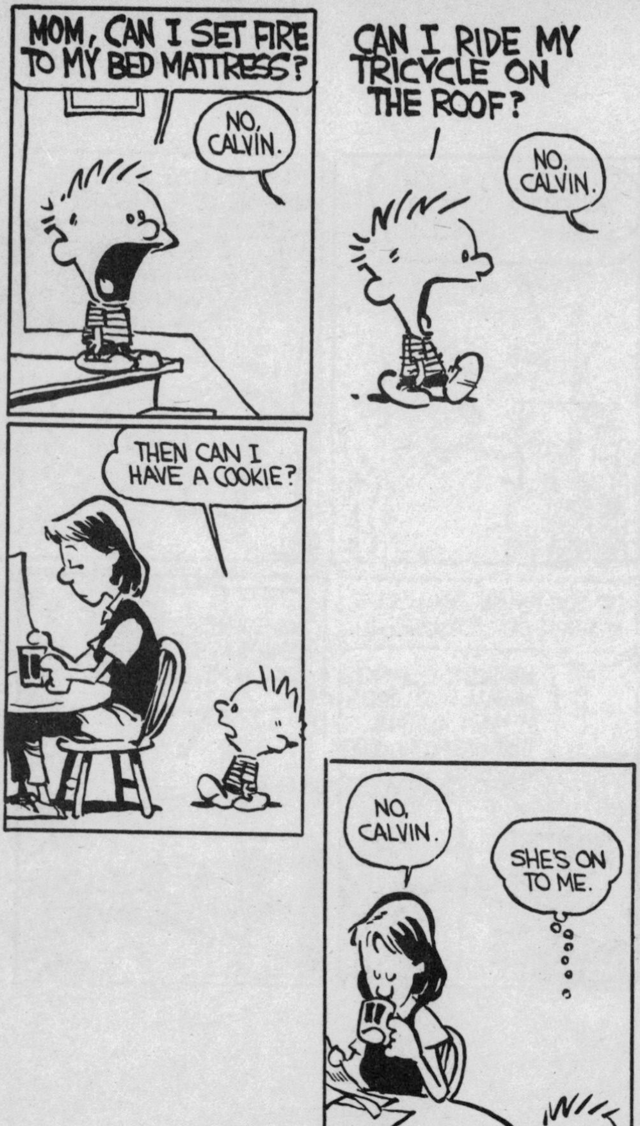
MOM, CAN I SET FIRE TO MY BED MATTRESS?
NO, CALVIN.
CAN I RIDE MY TRICYCLE ON THE ROOF?
NO, CALVIN.
THEN CAN I HAVE A COOKIE?
NO, CALVIN.
SHE'S ON TO ME.
WATTERSON

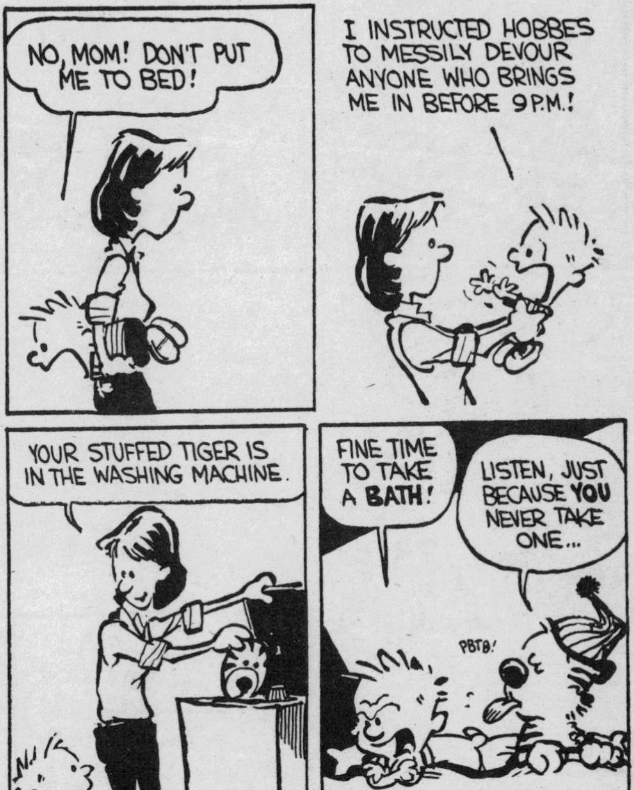
NO, MOM! DON'T PUT ME TO BED!
I INSTRUCTED HOBBES TO MESSILY DEVOUR ANYONE WHO BRINGS ME IN BEFORE 9 P.M.!
YOUR STUFFED TIGER IS IN THE WASHING MACHINE.
FINE TIME TO TAKE A BATH!
LISTEN, JUST BECAUSE YOU NEVER TAKE ONE...
PBTB!
WATTERSON

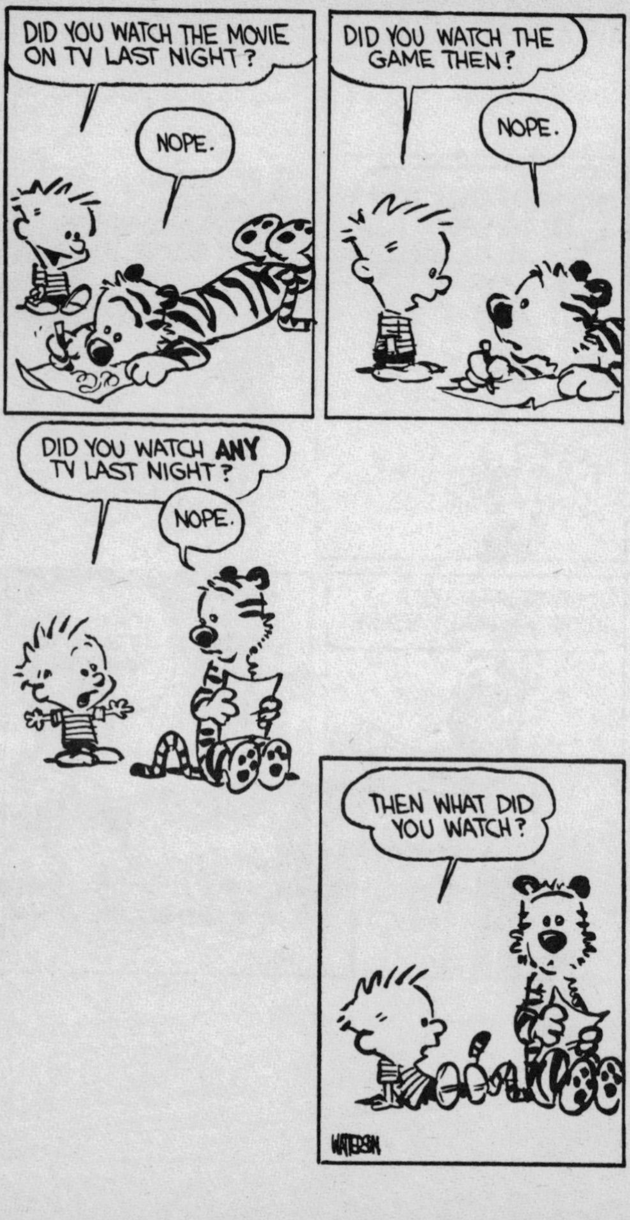
DID YOU WATCH THE MOVIE ON TV LAST NIGHT?
NOPE.
DID YOU WATCH THE GAME THEN?
NOPE.
DID YOU WATCH ANY TV LAST NIGHT?
NOPE.
THEN WHAT DID YOU WATCH?
WATERSON

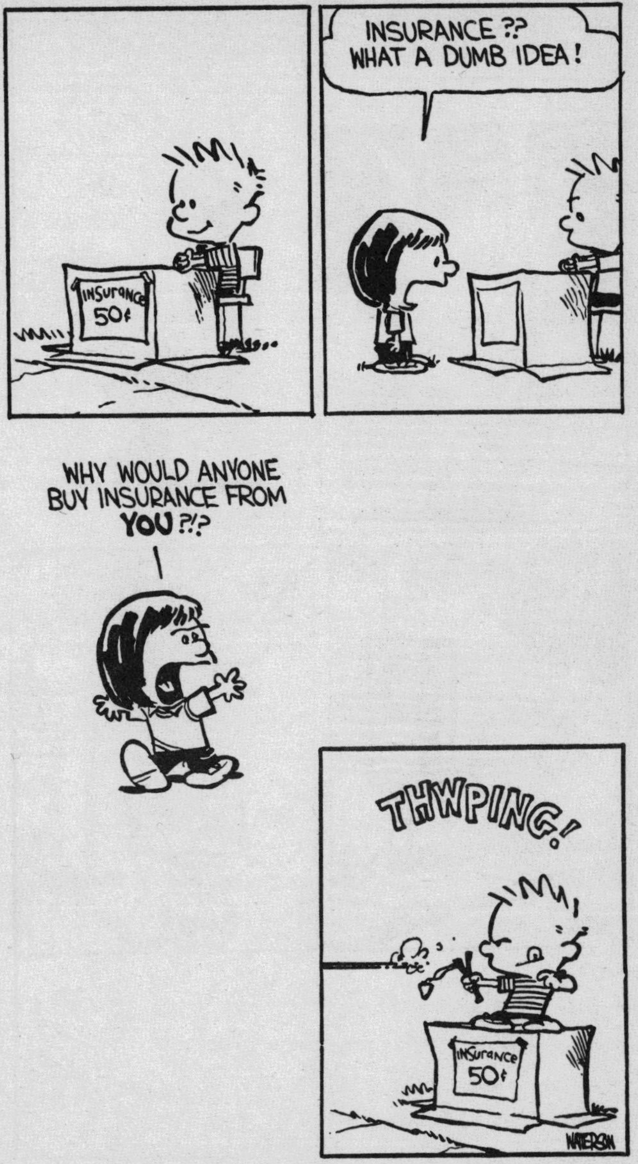
Insurance 50¢
INSURANCE ?? WHAT A DUMB IDEA!
WHY WOULD ANYONE BUY INSURANCE FROM YOU ?!?
THWPING!
Insurance 50¢

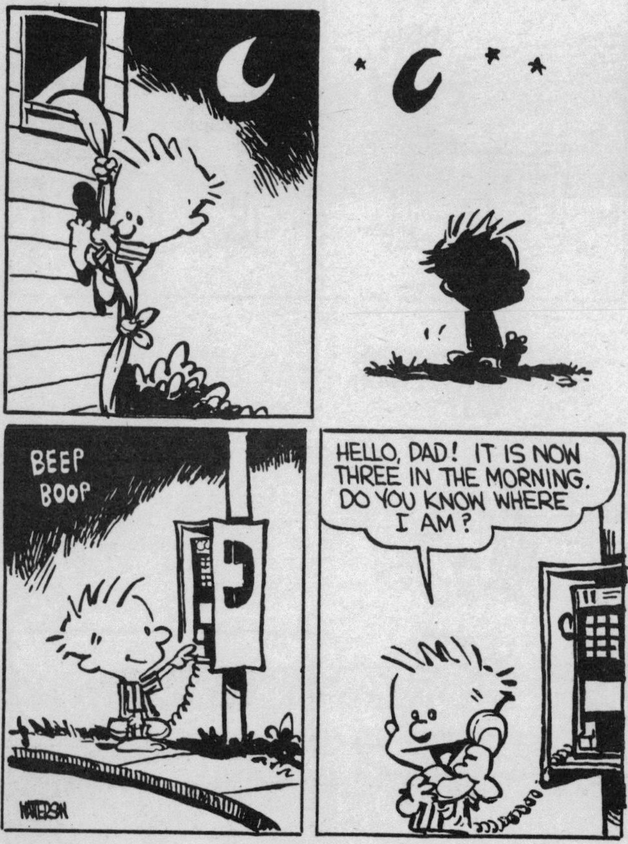
BEEP
BOOP
WATTERSON
HELLO, DAD! IT IS NOW THREE IN THE MORNING. DO YOU KNOW WHERE I AM?

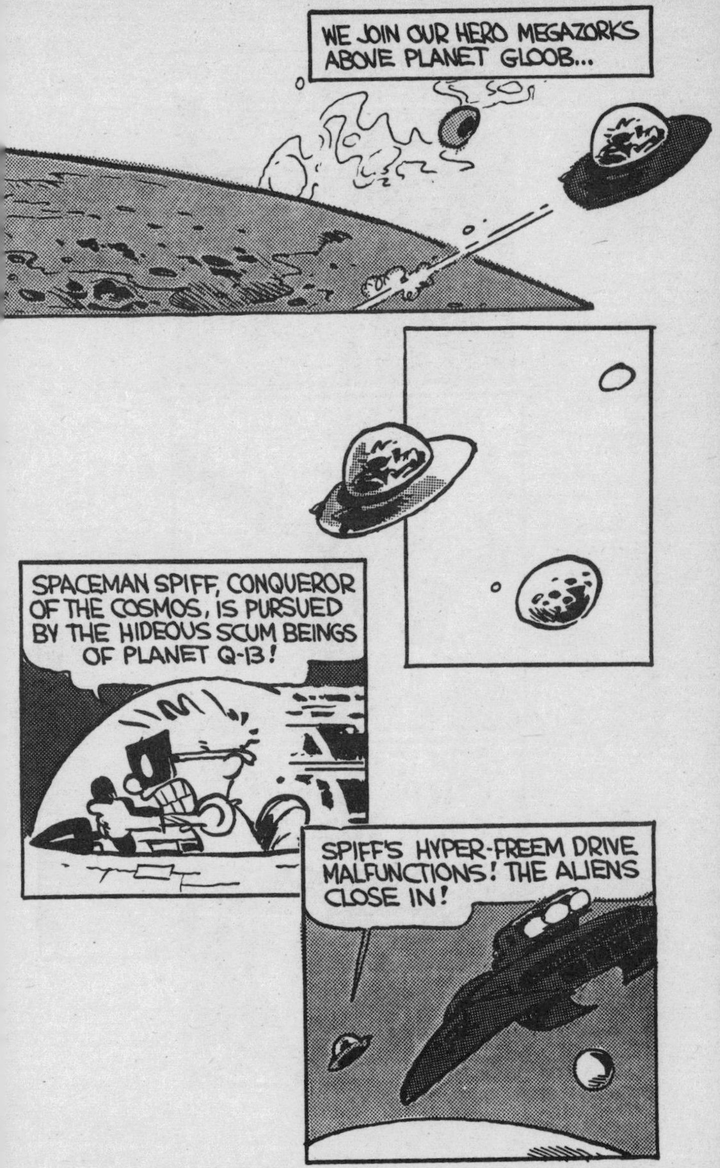
WE JOIN OUR HERO MEGAZORKS ABOVE PLANET GLOOB...
SPACEMAN SPIFF, CONQUEROR OF THE COSMOS, IS PURSUED BY THE HIDEOUS SCUM BEINGS OF PLANET Q-13!
SPIFF'S HYPER-FREEM DRIVE MALFUNCTIONS! THE ALIENS CLOSE IN!

SUDDENLY, A SEARING BOLT OF DEADLY FRAP RAY SLICES ACROSS THE BLACKNESS! OUR HERO IS UNFAZED.
ANOTHER BOLT! SPIFF IS HIT!!
PLOOIE!
SPIFF IS GOING DOWN! CAN HE MAKE IT?? IS THIS THE END?!?

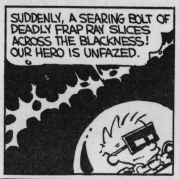

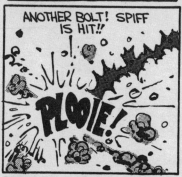

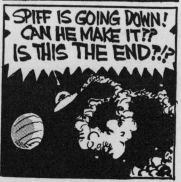

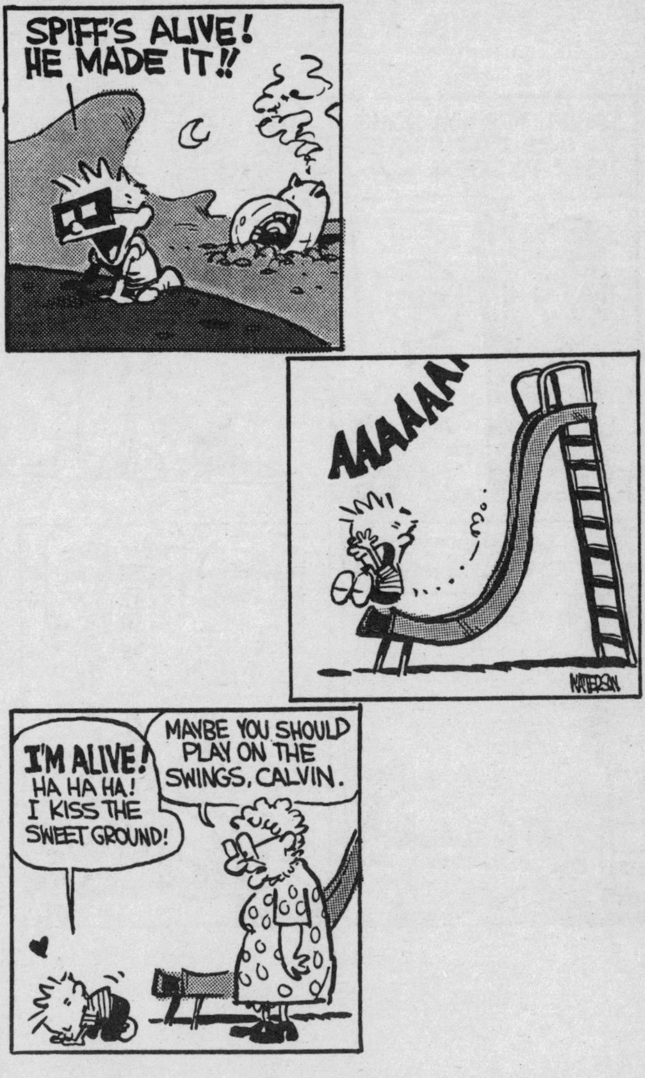
SPIFF'S ALIVE! HE MADE IT!!
AAAAA
I'M ALIVE! HA HA HA! I KISS THE SWEET GROUND!
MAYBE YOU SHOULD PLAY ON THE SWINGS, CALVIN.

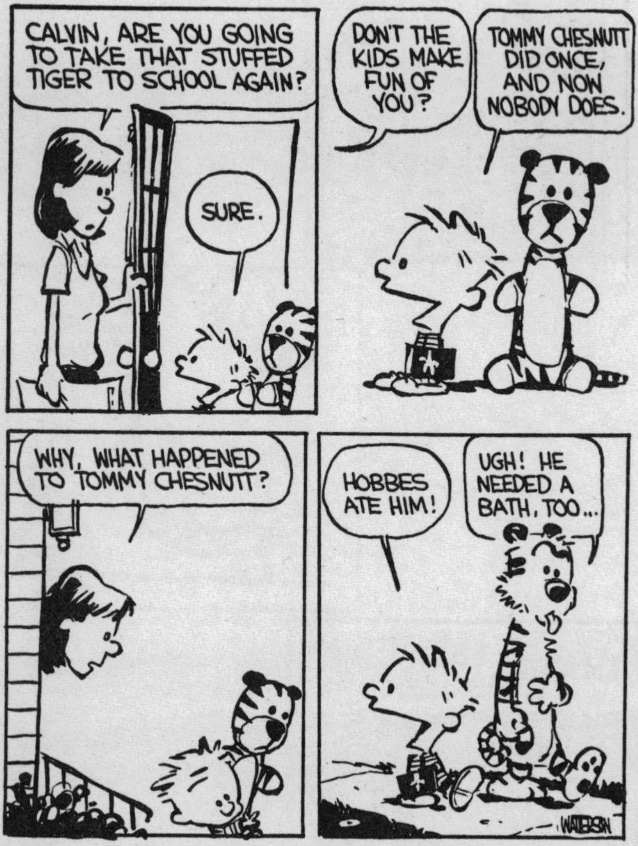
CALVIN, ARE YOU GOING TO TAKE THAT STUFFED TIGER TO SCHOOL AGAIN?
SURE.
DON'T THE KIDS MAKE FUN OF YOU?
TOMMY CHESNUTT DID ONCE, AND NOW NOBODY DOES.
WHY, WHAT HAPPENED TO TOMMY CHESNUTT?
HOBBES ATE HIM!
UGH! HE NEEDED A BATH, TOO...
WATERSON

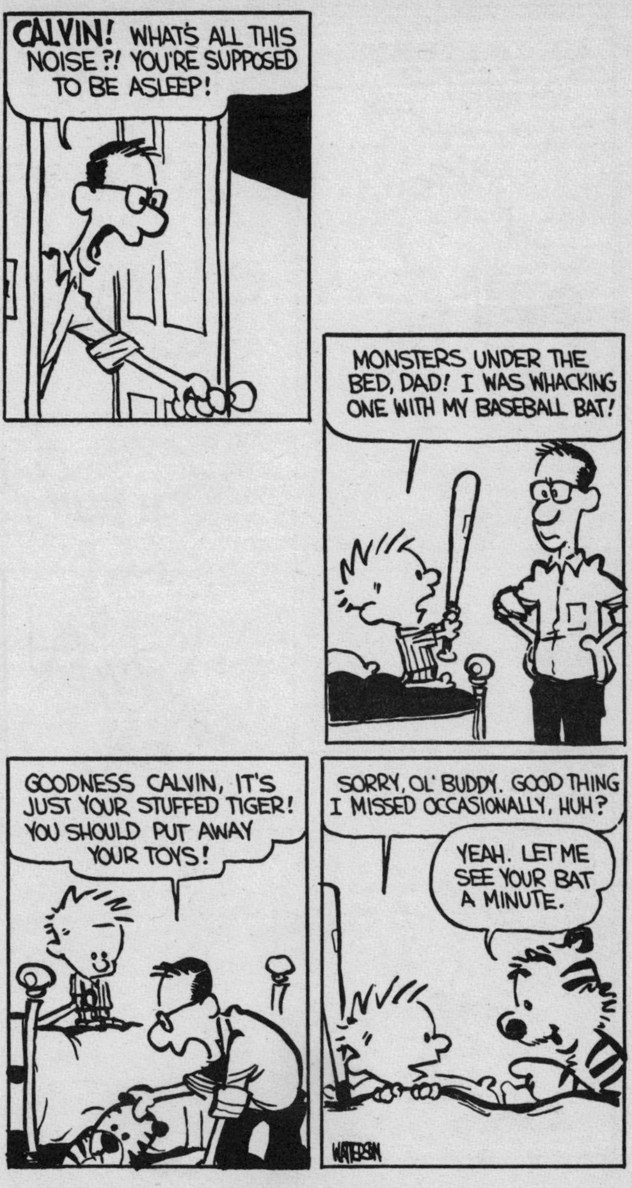
CALVIN! WHAT'S ALL THIS NOISE ?! YOU'RE SUPPOSED TO BE ASLEEP!
MONSTERS UNDER THE BED, DAD! I WAS WHACKING ONE WITH MY BASEBALL BAT!
GOODNESS CALVIN, IT'S JUST YOUR STUFFED TIGER! YOU SHOULD PUT AWAY YOUR TOYS!
SORRY, OL' BUDDY. GOOD THING I MISSED OCCASIONALLY, HUH?
YEAH. LET ME SEE YOUR BAT A MINUTE.
WATERSON

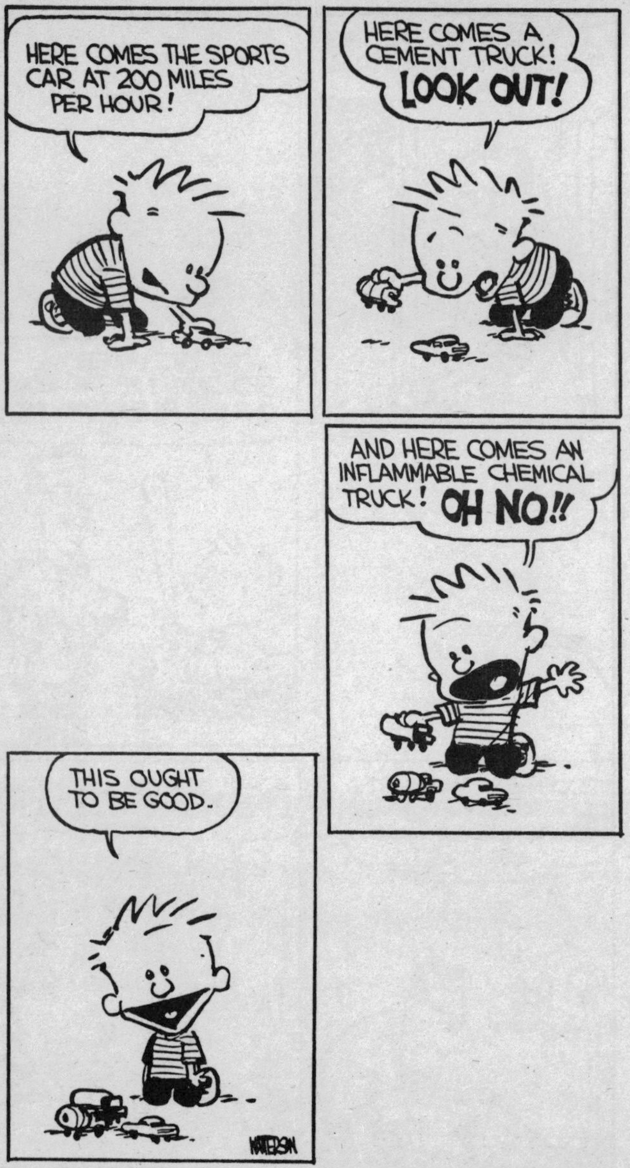
HERE COMES THE SPORTS CAR AT 200 MILES PER HOUR!
HERE COMES A CEMENT TRUCK! LOOK OUT!
AND HERE COMES AN INFLAMMABLE CHEMICAL TRUCK! OH NO!!
THIS OUGHT TO BE GOOD.

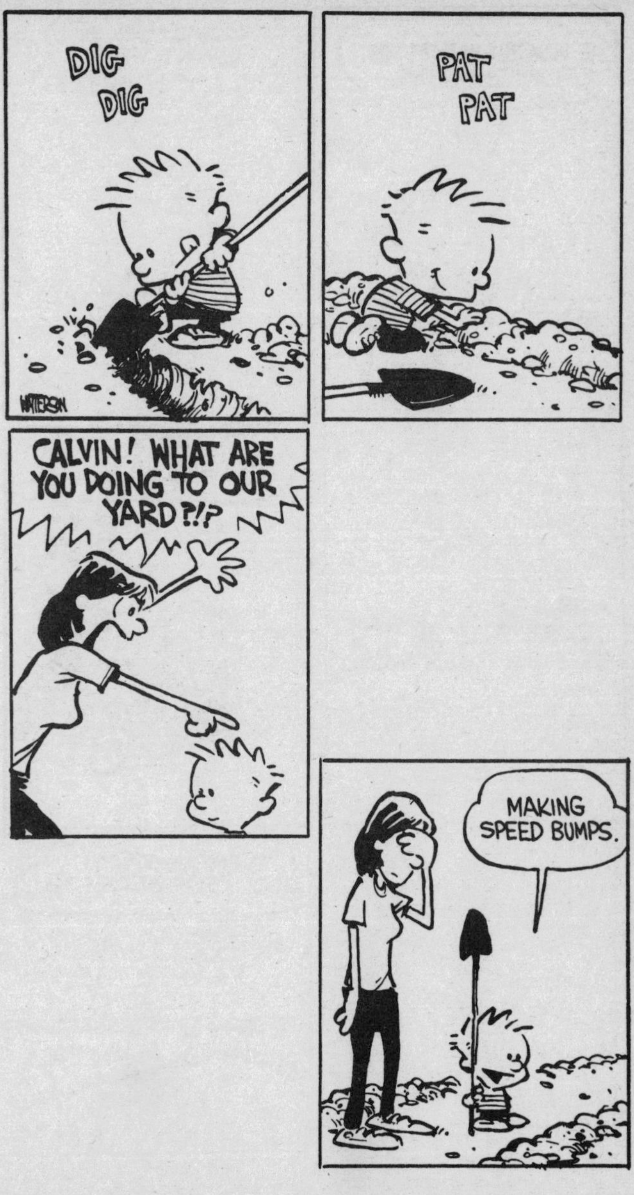
DIG DIG
WATTERSON
PAT PAT
CALVIN! WHAT ARE YOU DOING TO OUR YARD?!?
MAKING SPEED BUMPS.

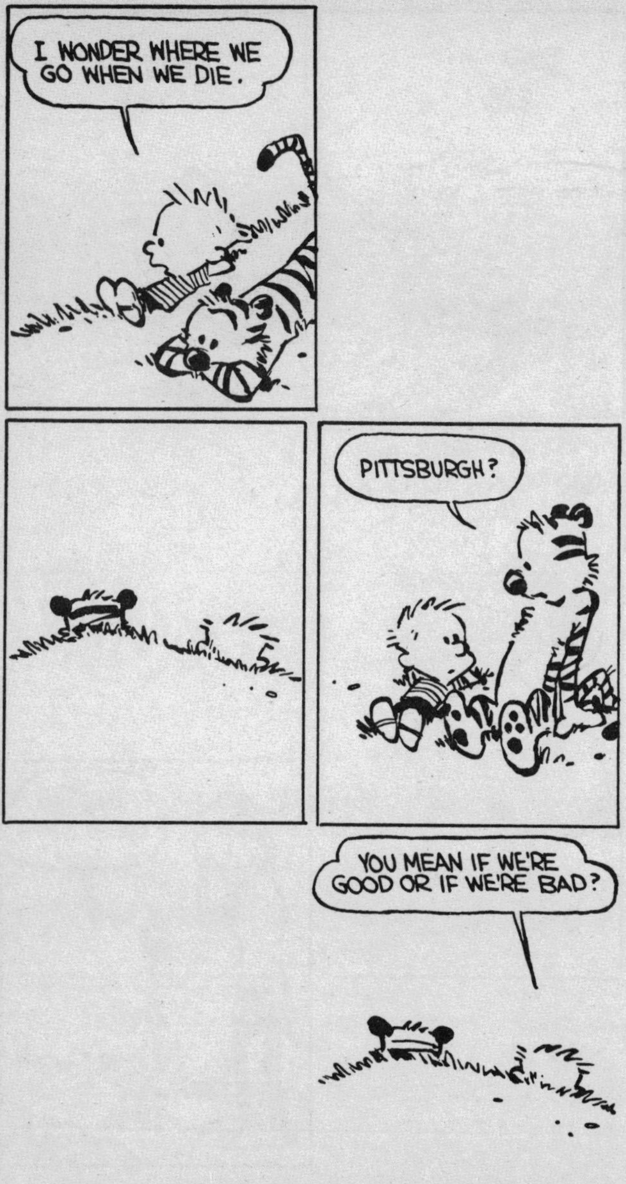
I WONDER WHERE WE GO WHEN WE DIE.
PITTSBURGH?
YOU MEAN IF WE'RE GOOD OR IF WE'RE BAD?

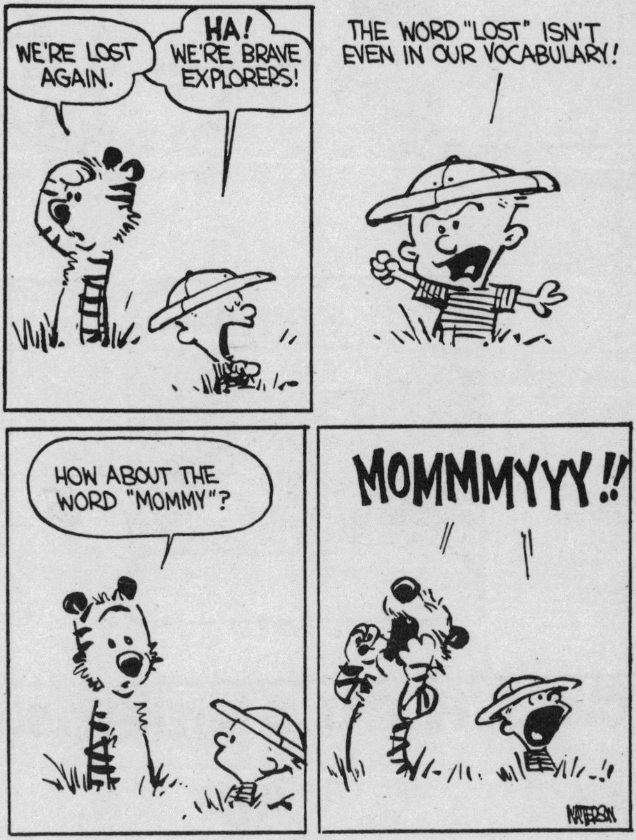
WE'RE LOST AGAIN.
HA! WE'RE BRAVE EXPLORERS!
THE WORD "LOST" ISN'T EVEN IN OUR VOCABULARY!
HOW ABOUT THE WORD "MOMMY"?
MOMMMYYY!!
WATTERSON

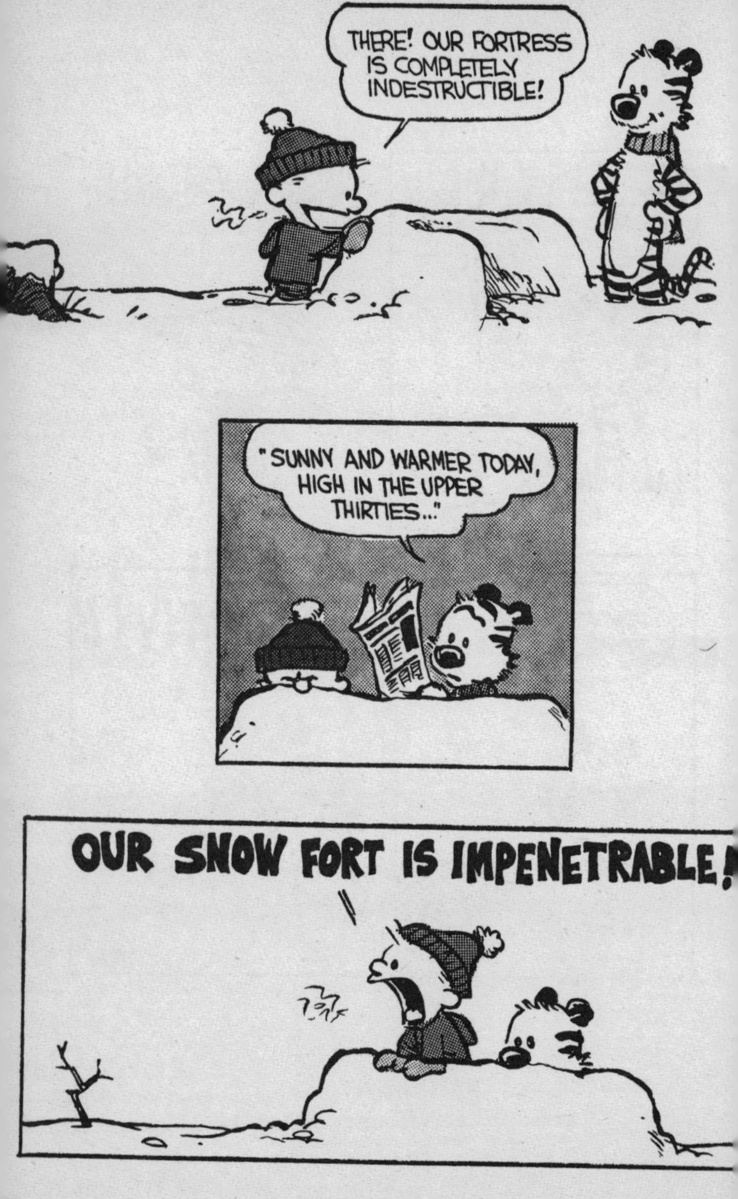
THERE! OUR FORTRESS IS COMPLETELY INDESTRUCTIBLE!
"SUNNY AND WARMER TODAY, HIGH IN THE UPPER THIRTIES..."
OUR SNOW FORT IS IMPENETRABLE!

AT THE SLIGHTEST PROVOCATION, WE'LL LET LOOSE A MERCILESS BARRAGE OF STINGING ICE!!
NONE DARE ATTACK US! WE RULE ALL!!
TOGETHER, A VERITABLE FIST OF DEFIANCE, WE STAND IMMUNE TO ANY ONSLAUGHT!

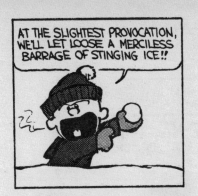

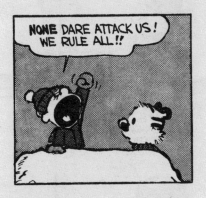

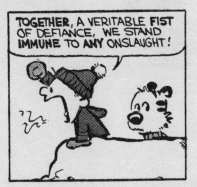

WE ARE INVINCIBLE!!
WE...UH...UMM..
I
PIFF!

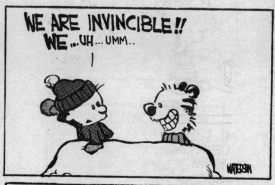

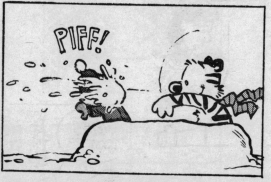

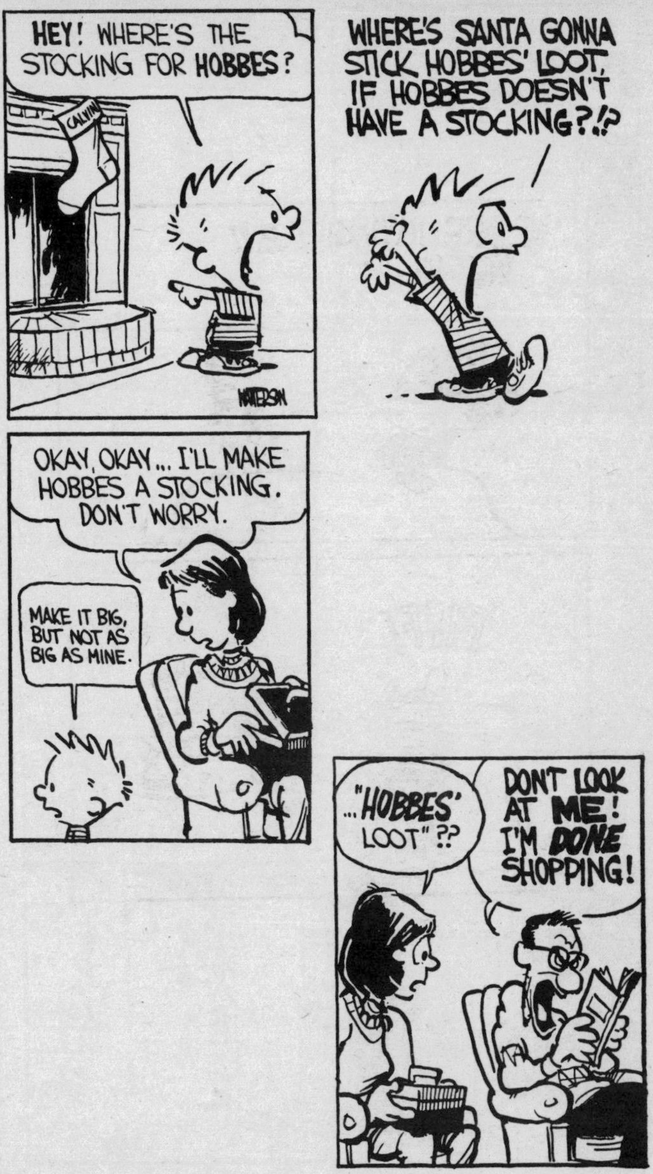

HEY! WHERE'S THE STOCKING FOR HOBBES?
CALVIN
WATTERSON
WHERE'S SANTA GONNA STICK HOBBES' LOOT, IF HOBBES DOESN'T HAVE A STOCKING?!?
OKAY, OKAY... I'LL MAKE HOBBES A STOCKING. DON'T WORRY.
MAKE IT BIG, BUT NOT AS BIG AS MINE.
..."HOBBES' LOOT"??
DON'T LOOK AT ME! I'M DONE SHOPPING!

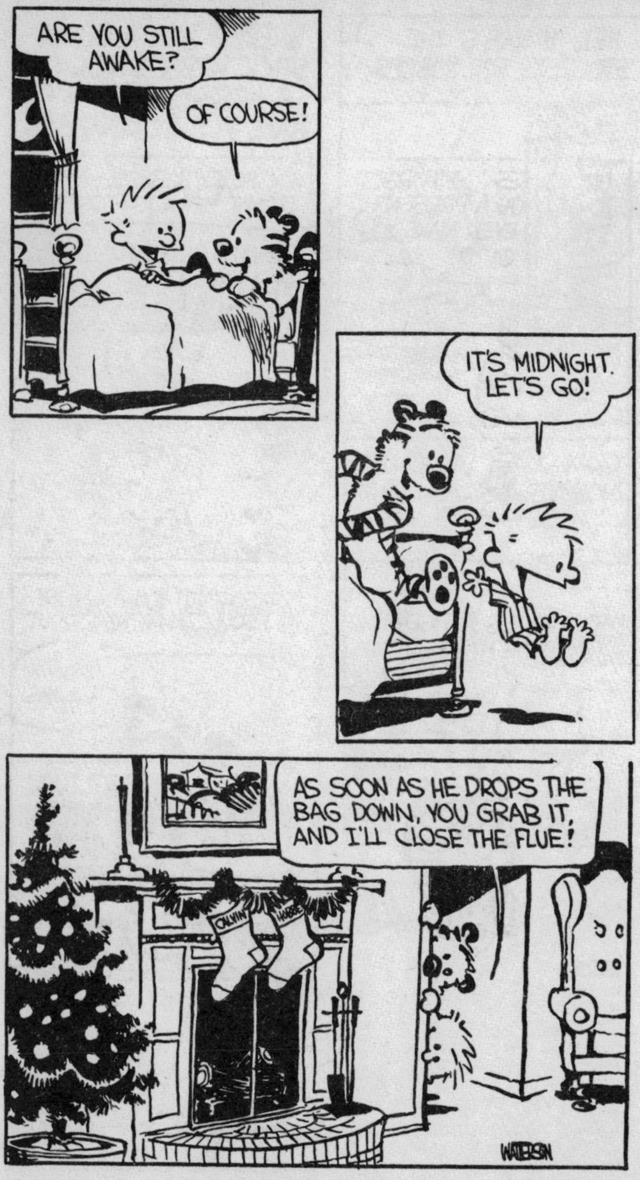
ARE YOU STILL AWAKE?
OF COURSE!
IT'S MIDNIGHT. LET'S GO!
AS SOON AS HE DROPS THE BAG DOWN, YOU GRAB IT, AND I'LL CLOSE THE FLUE!
CALVIN
WATTERSON

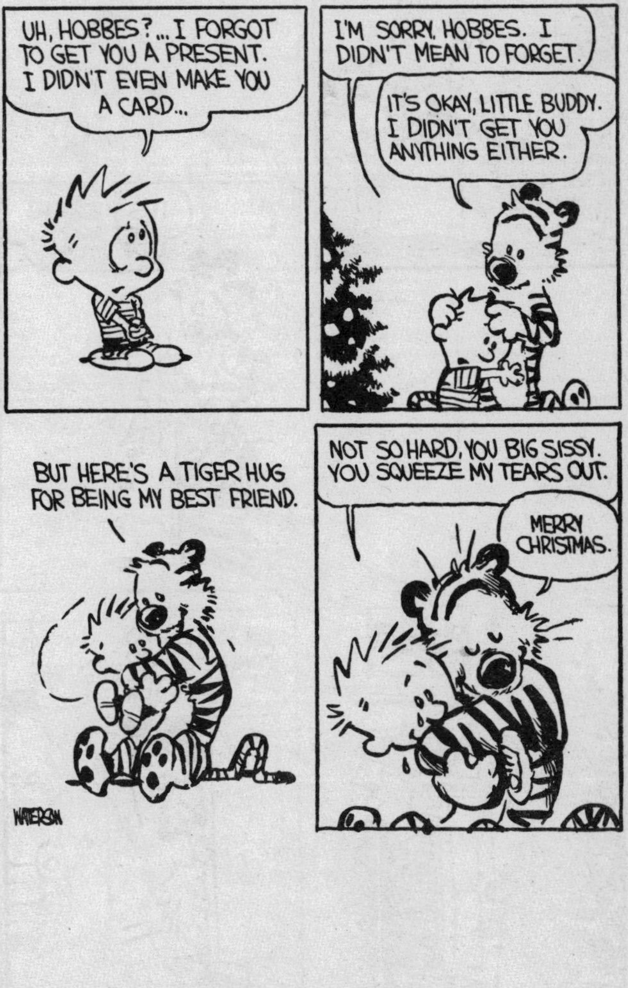
UH, HOBBES?... I FORGOT TO GET YOU A PRESENT. I DIDN'T EVEN MAKE YOU A CARD...
I'M SORRY, HOBBES. I DIDN'T MEAN TO FORGET.
IT'S OKAY, LITTLE BUDDY. I DIDN'T GET YOU ANYTHING EITHER.
BUT HERE'S A TIGER HUG FOR BEING MY BEST FRIEND.
NOT SO HARD, YOU BIG SISSY. YOU SQUEEZE MY TEARS OUT.
MERRY CHRISTMAS.
WATERSON

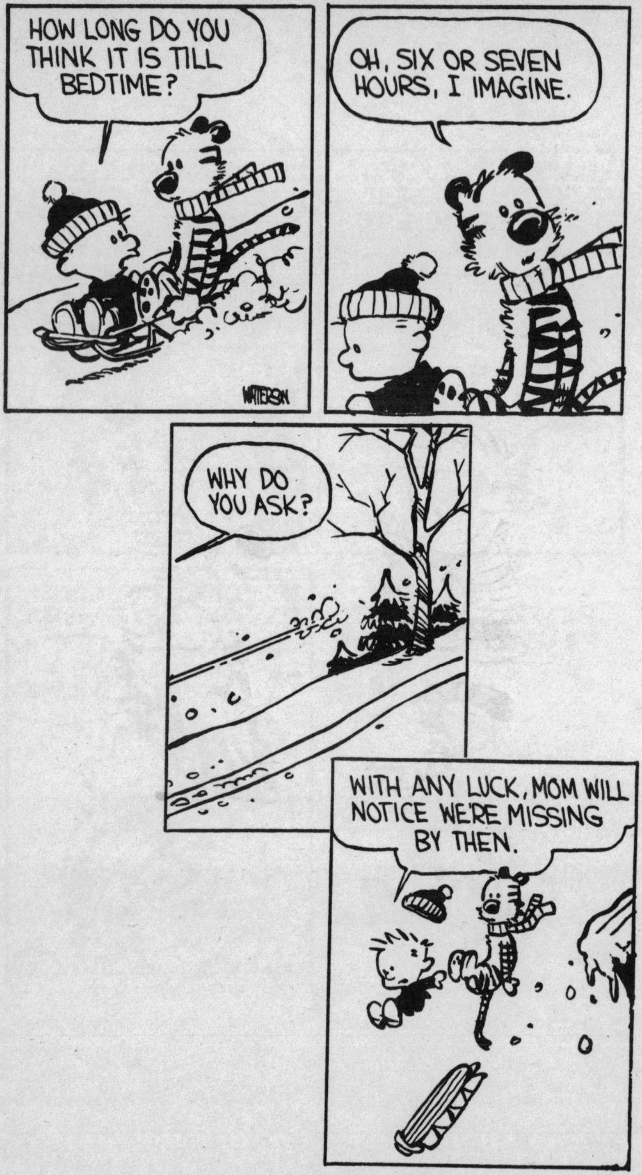
HOW LONG DO YOU THINK IT IS TILL BEDTIME?
WATTERSON
OH, SIX OR SEVEN HOURS, I IMAGINE.
WHY DO YOU ASK?
WITH ANY LUCK, MOM WILL NOTICE WE'RE MISSING BY THEN.

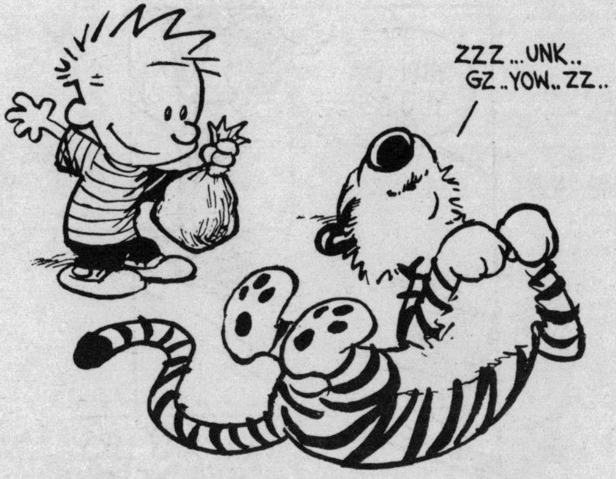
ZZZ...UNK..
GZ..YOW..ZZ..

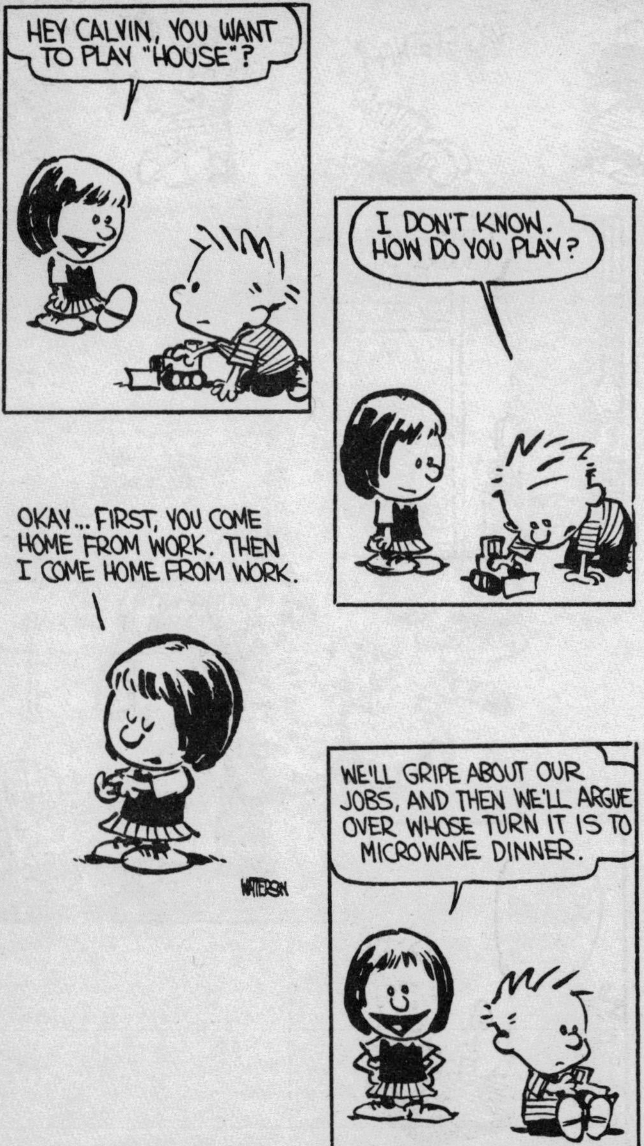
HEY CALVIN, YOU WANT TO PLAY "HOUSE"?
I DON'T KNOW. HOW DO YOU PLAY?
OKAY... FIRST, YOU COME HOME FROM WORK. THEN I COME HOME FROM WORK.
WE'LL GRIPE ABOUT OUR JOBS, AND THEN WE'LL ARGUE OVER WHOSE TURN IT IS TO MICROWAVE DINNER.
WATTERSON

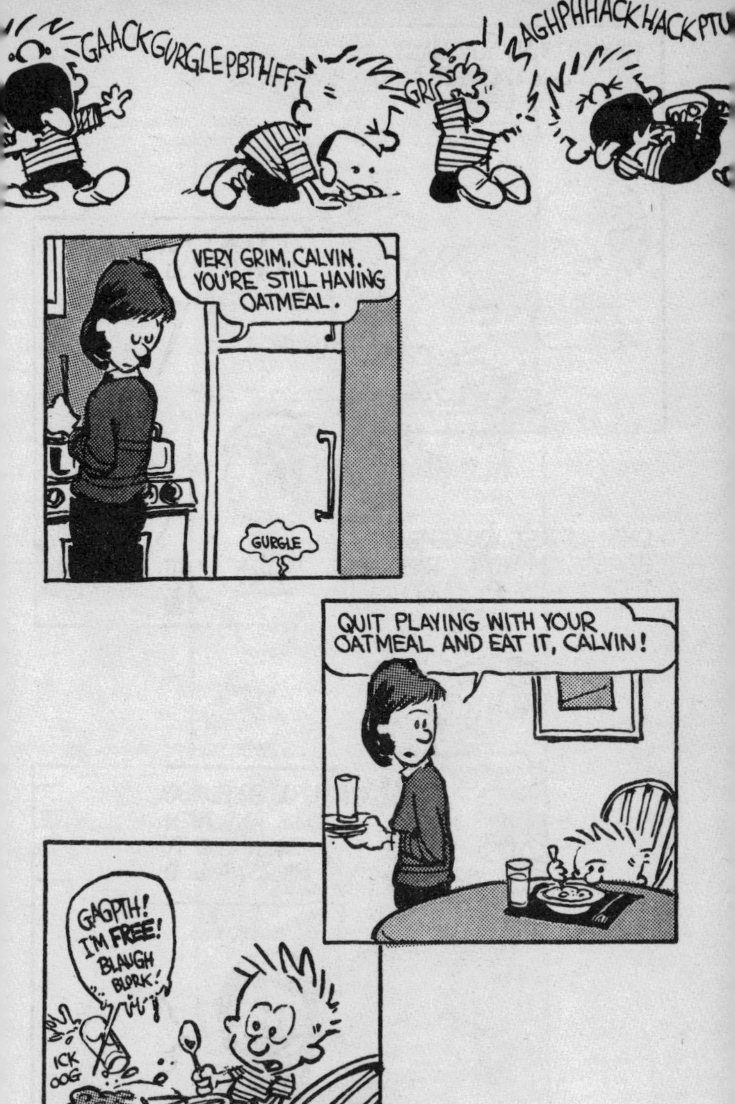
GAACK GURGLE PBTHFF
GR!
AGHPHHACK HACK PTU
VERY GRIM, CALVIN. YOU'RE STILL HAVING OATMEAL.
GURGLE
QUIT PLAYING WITH YOUR OATMEAL AND EAT IT, CALVIN!
GAGPTH! I'M FREE! BLAUGH BLORK!
ICK OOG

YAAH! DEATH TO OATMEAL!
KACHUNK!
NGH
BLOOP
ORG
YOU'LL NEVER ESCAPE, VILE GLOP! DIE! DIE!
ORK
IG
GOOK
CALVIN! QUIT...
..OH NO....

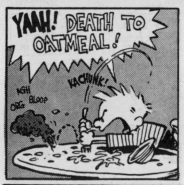

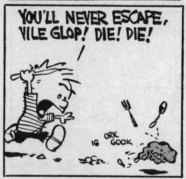

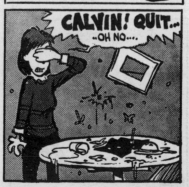

IT'S YOUR FAULT WE DIDN'T HAVE A SWEET LITTLE GIRL! YOUR STUPID CHROMOSOME!! NOT MINE!!
...I JUST LIVE HERE...
WATTERSON

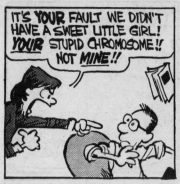

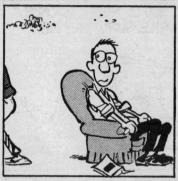

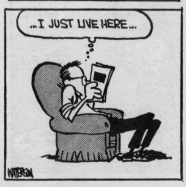

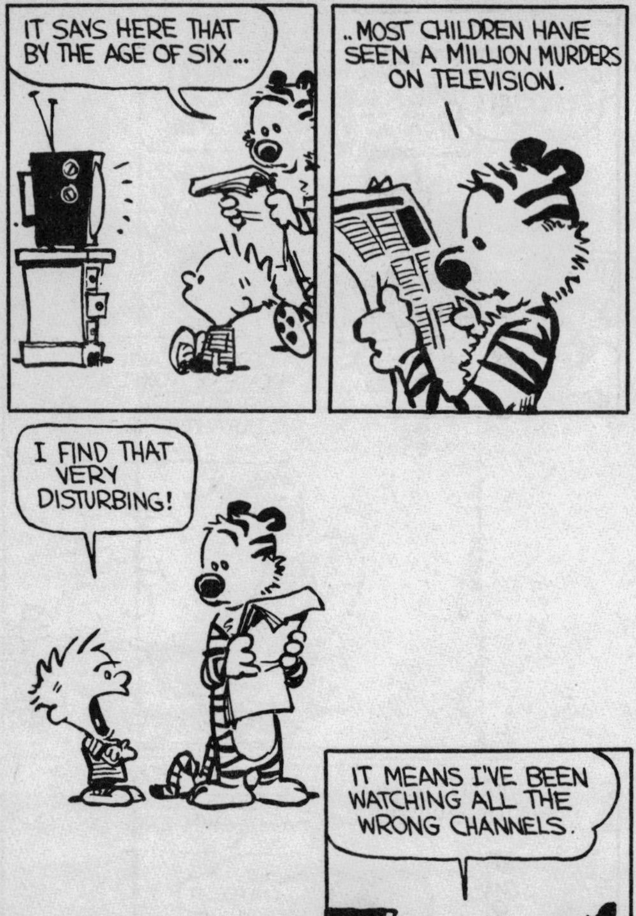
IT SAYS HERE THAT BY THE AGE OF SIX ...
.. MOST CHILDREN HAVE SEEN A MILLION MURDERS ON TELEVISION.
I FIND THAT VERY DISTURBING!
IT MEANS I'VE BEEN WATCHING ALL THE WRONG CHANNELS.
WATERSON

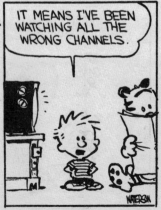

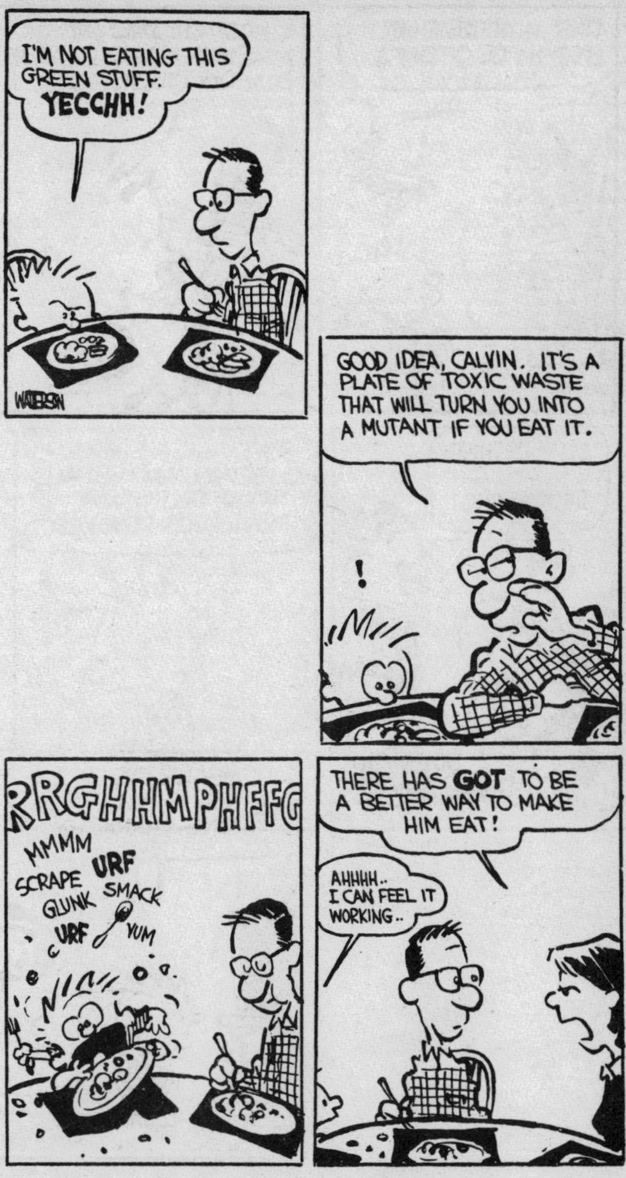
I'M NOT EATING THIS GREEN STUFF. YECCHH!
GOOD IDEA, CALVIN. IT'S A PLATE OF TOXIC WASTE THAT WILL TURN YOU INTO A MUTANT IF YOU EAT IT.
!
RRGHHMPHFFG
MMMM
URF
SCRAPE
SMACK
GLUNK
URF
YUM
THERE HAS GOT TO BE A BETTER WAY TO MAKE HIM EAT!
AHHHH.. I CAN FEEL IT WORKING..

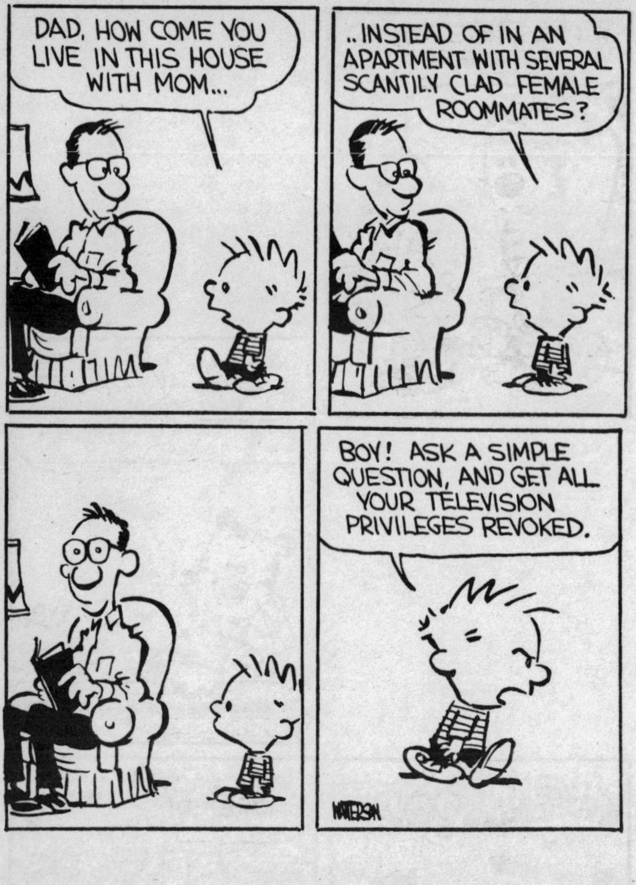
DAD, HOW COME YOU LIVE IN THIS HOUSE WITH MOM...
..INSTEAD OF IN AN APARTMENT WITH SEVERAL SCANTILY CLAD FEMALE ROOMMATES?
BOY! ASK A SIMPLE QUESTION, AND GET ALL YOUR TELEVISION PRIVILEGES REVOKED.
WATERSON

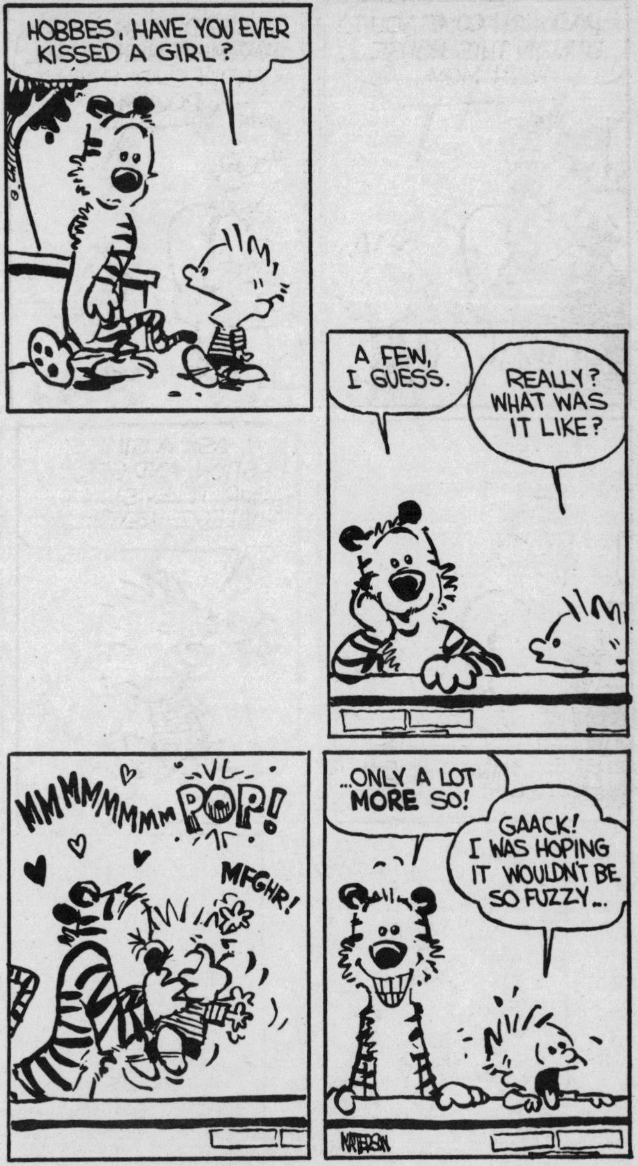
HOBBES, HAVE YOU EVER KISSED A GIRL?
A FEW, I GUESS.
REALLY? WHAT WAS IT LIKE?
MMMMMMMMM POP!
MFGHR!
...ONLY A LOT MORE SO!
GAACK! I WAS HOPING IT WOULDN'T BE SO FUZZY...
WATTERSON

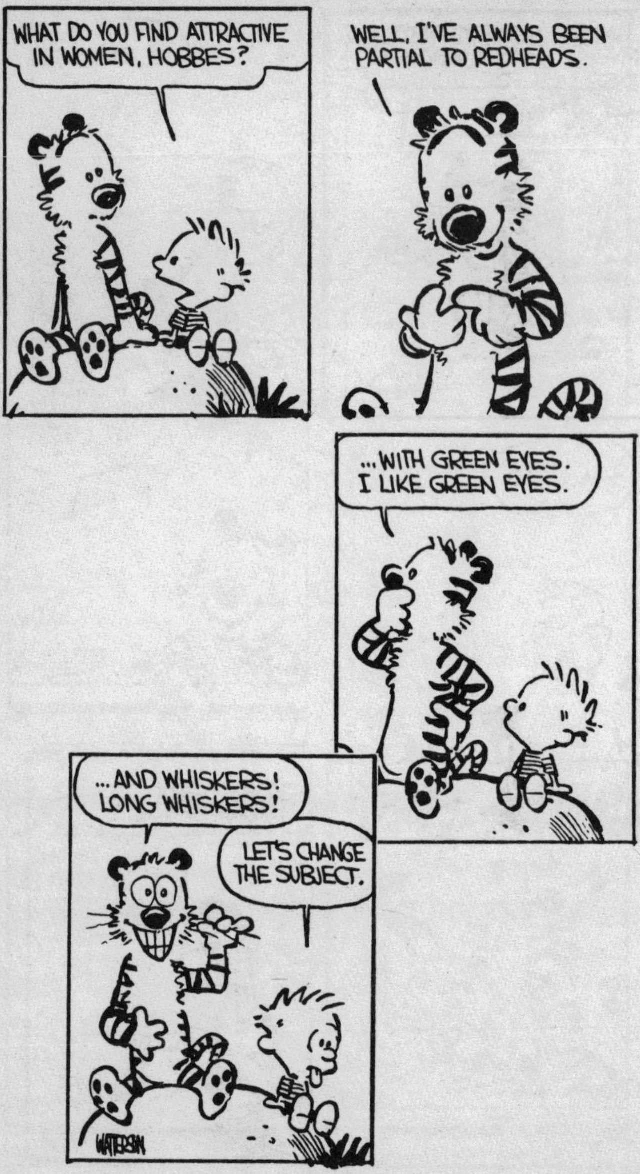
WHAT DO YOU FIND ATTRACTIVE IN WOMEN, HOBBES?
WELL, I'VE ALWAYS BEEN PARTIAL TO REDHEADS.
...WITH GREEN EYES. I LIKE GREEN EYES.
...AND WHISKERS! LONG WHISKERS!
LET'S CHANGE THE SUBJECT.
WATTERSON

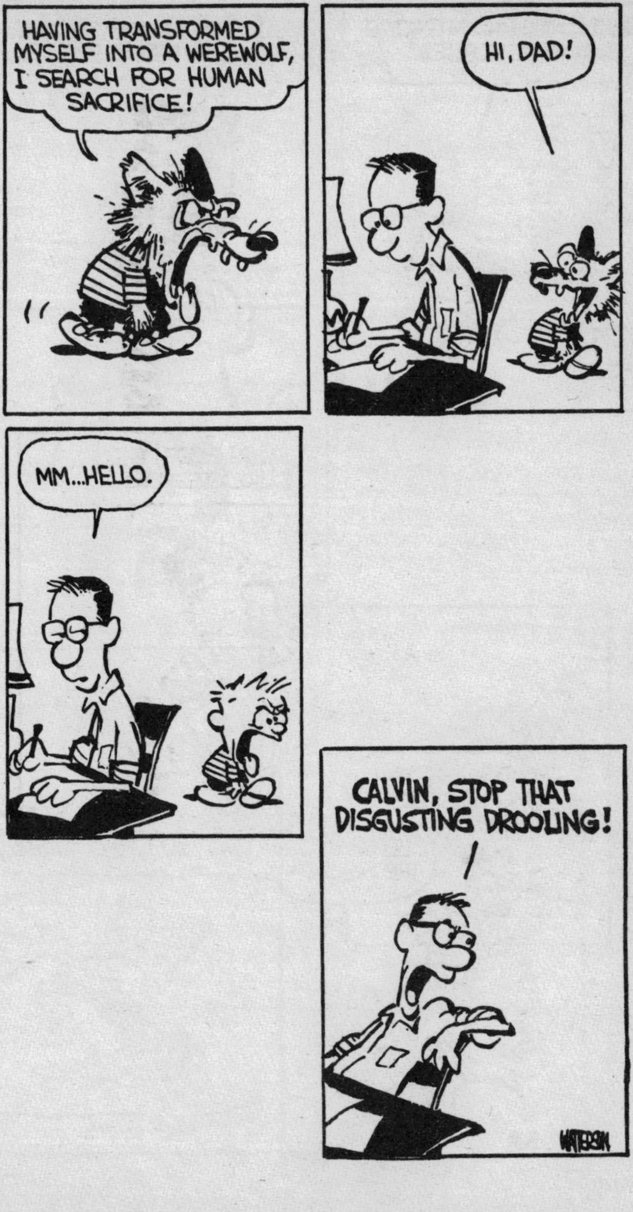
HAVING TRANSFORMED MYSELF INTO A WEREWOLF, I SEARCH FOR HUMAN SACRIFICE!
HI, DAD!
MM...HELLO.
CALVIN, STOP THAT DISGUSTING DROOLING!

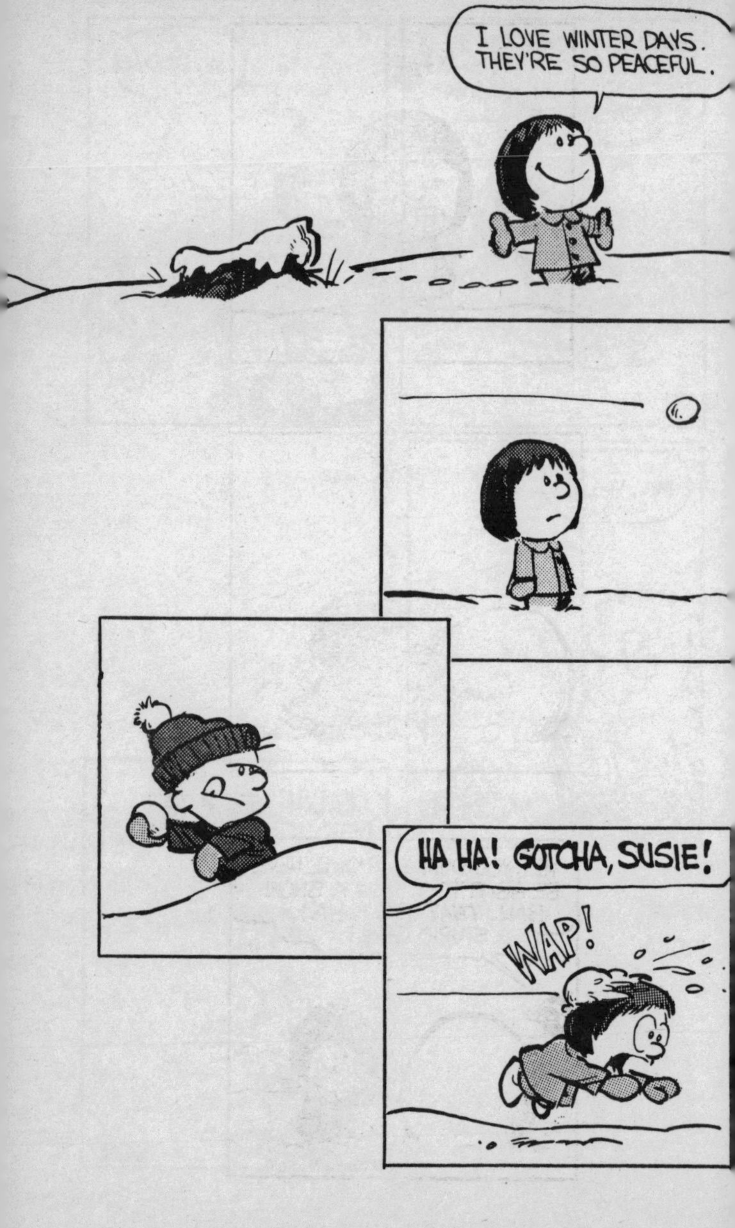
I LOVE WINTER DAYS. THEY'RE SO PEACEFUL.
HA HA! GOTCHA, SUSIE!
WAP!

HEY, YOU DUMMY! YOU'LL NEVER BE ABLE TO THROW A SNOW BALL *THAT* BIG! HA! STUPID GIRL!

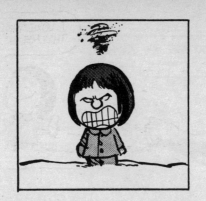

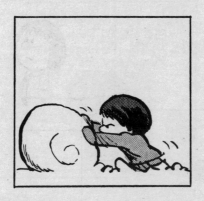

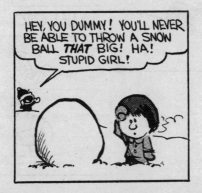

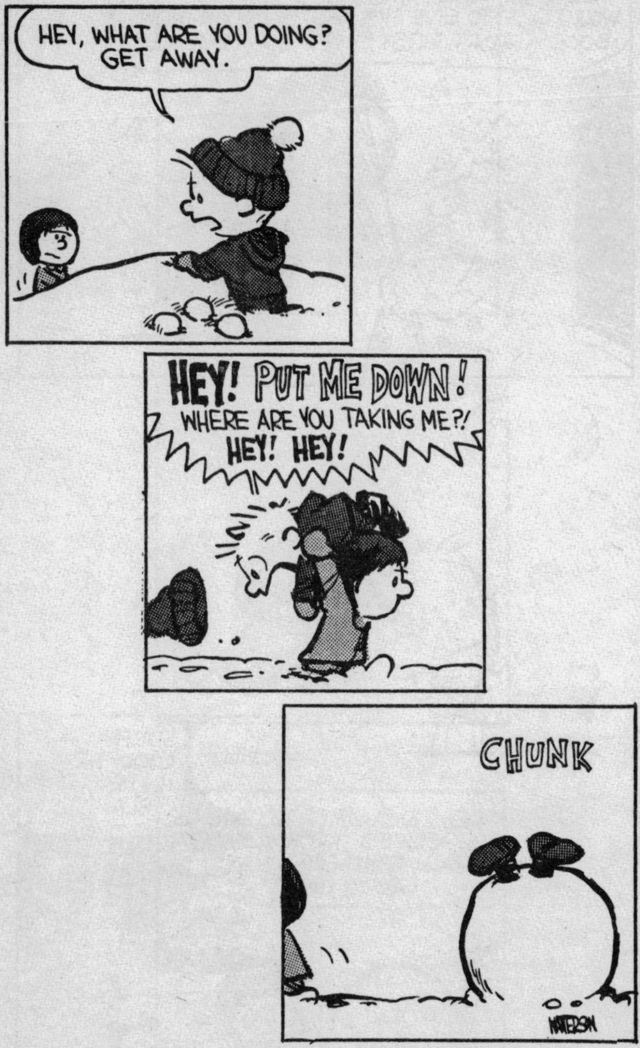
HEY, WHAT ARE YOU DOING? GET AWAY.
HEY! PUT ME DOWN! WHERE ARE YOU TAKING ME?! HEY! HEY!
CHUNK
WATERSON

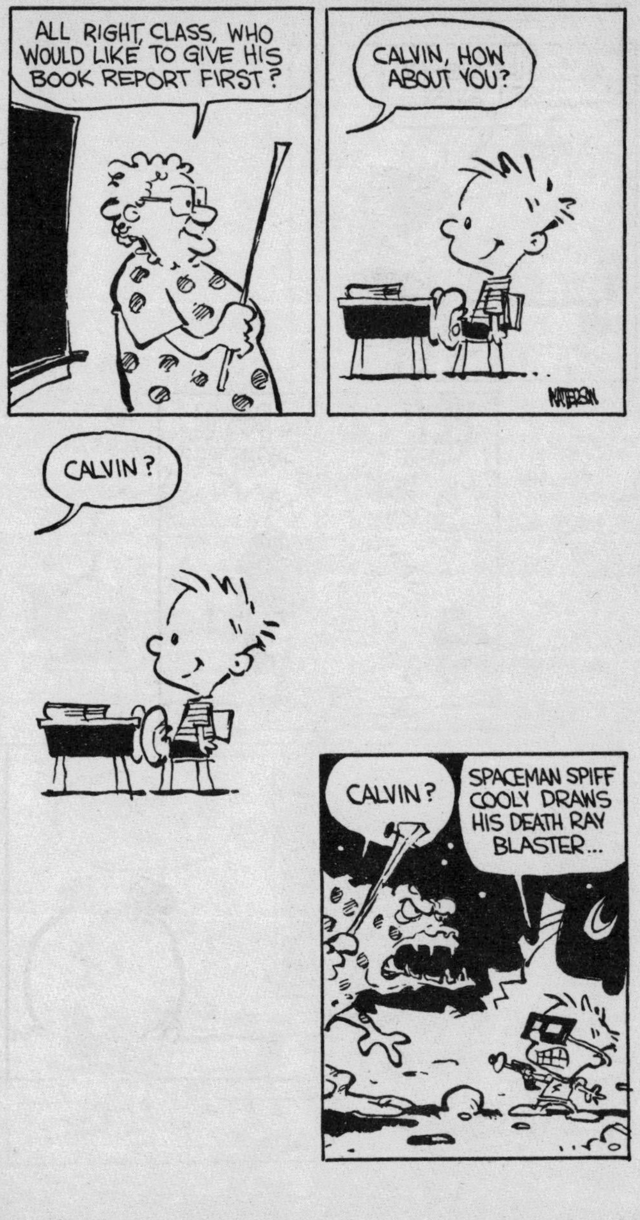
ALL RIGHT, CLASS, WHO WOULD LIKE TO GIVE HIS BOOK REPORT FIRST?
CALVIN, HOW ABOUT YOU?
CALVIN?
CALVIN?
SPACEMAN SPIFF COOLY DRAWS HIS DEATH RAY BLASTER...

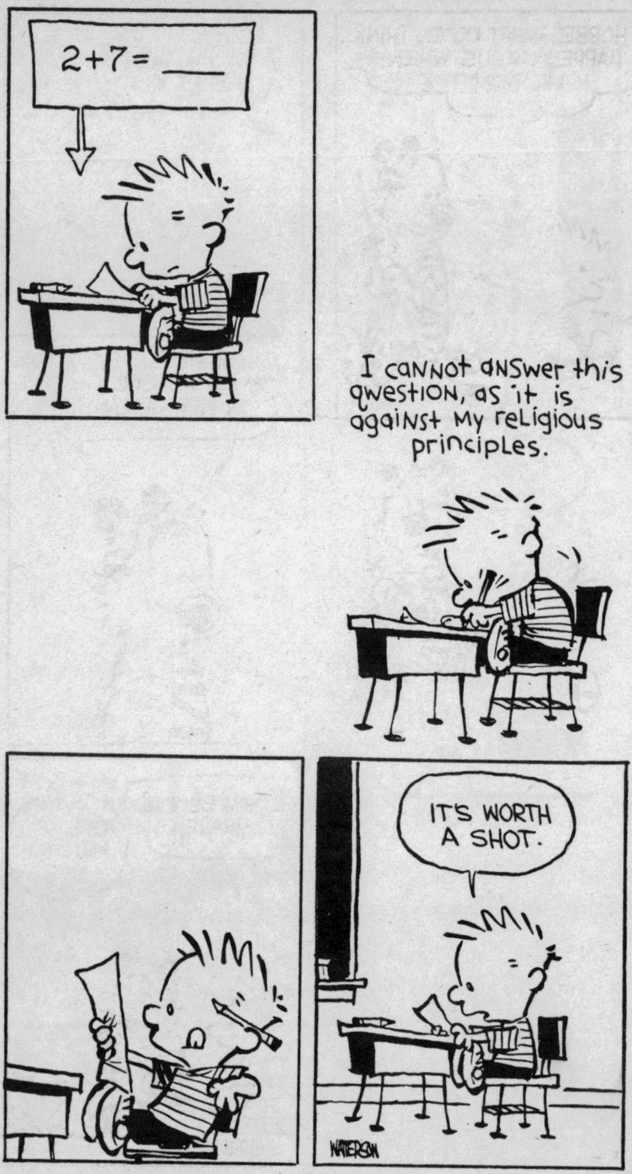
2+7= ____
I cannot answer this qwestion, as it is against my religious principles.
IT'S WORTH A SHOT.
WATERSON

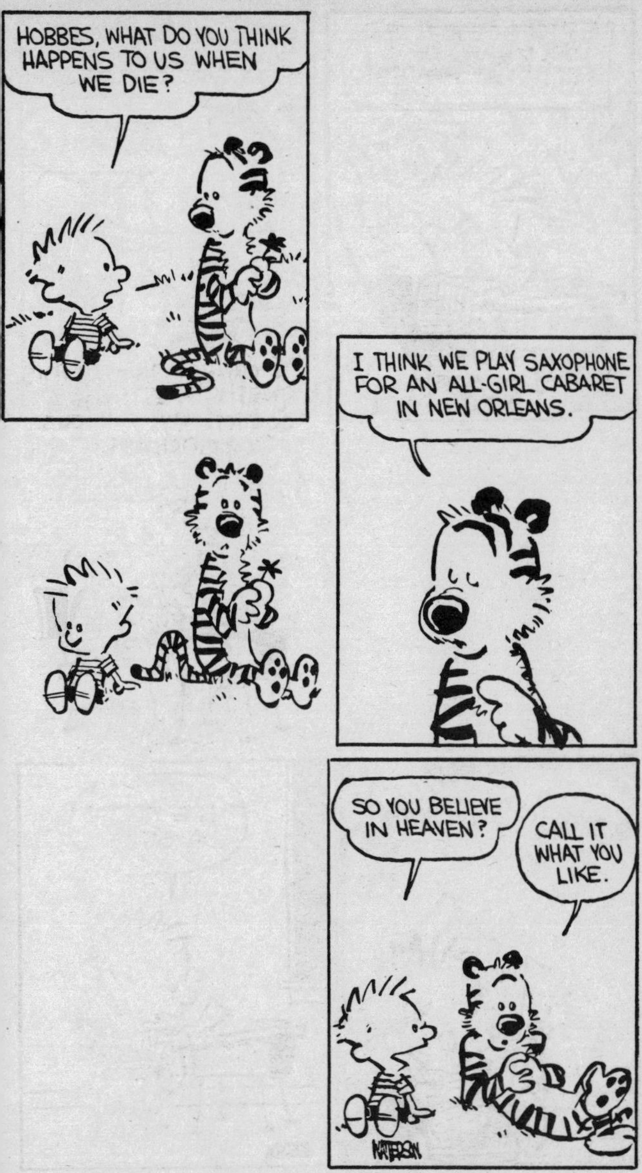

HOBBES, WHAT DO YOU THINK HAPPENS TO US WHEN WE DIE?
I THINK WE PLAY SAXOPHONE FOR AN ALL-GIRL CABARET IN NEW ORLEANS.
SO YOU BELIEVE IN HEAVEN?
CALL IT WHAT YOU LIKE.
WATTERSON

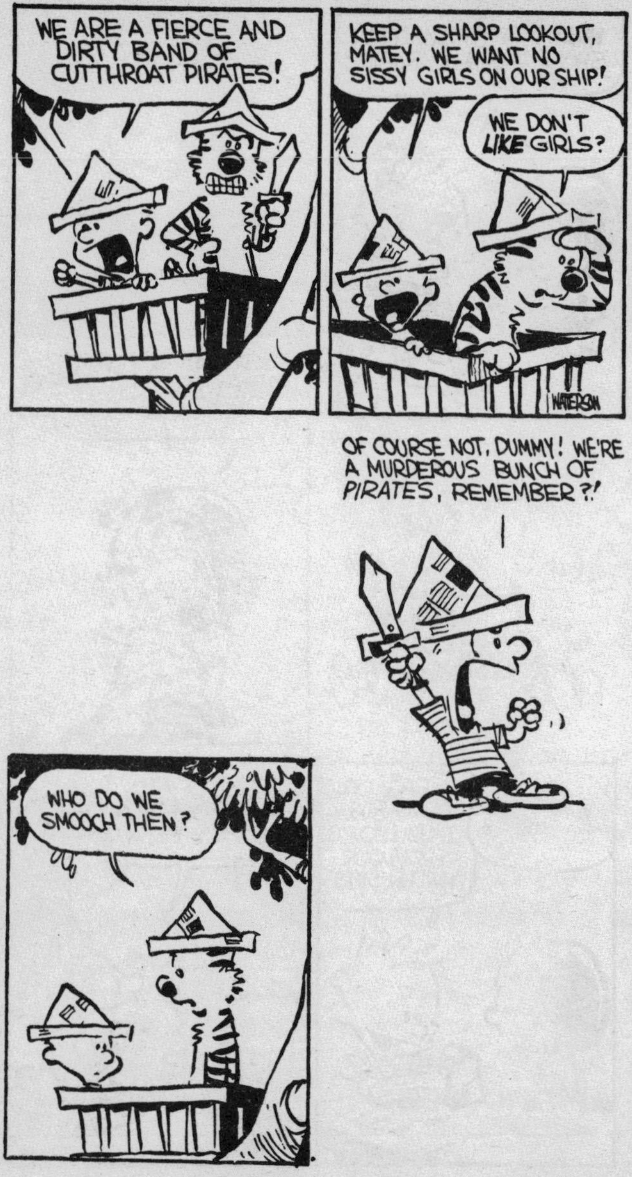

WE ARE A FIERCE AND DIRTY BAND OF CUTTHROAT PIRATES!
KEEP A SHARP LOOKOUT, MATEY. WE WANT NO SISSY GIRLS ON OUR SHIP!
WE DON'T LIKE GIRLS?
WATERSON
OF COURSE NOT, DUMMY! WE'RE A MURDEROUS BUNCH OF PIRATES, REMEMBER?!
WHO DO WE SMOOCH THEN?

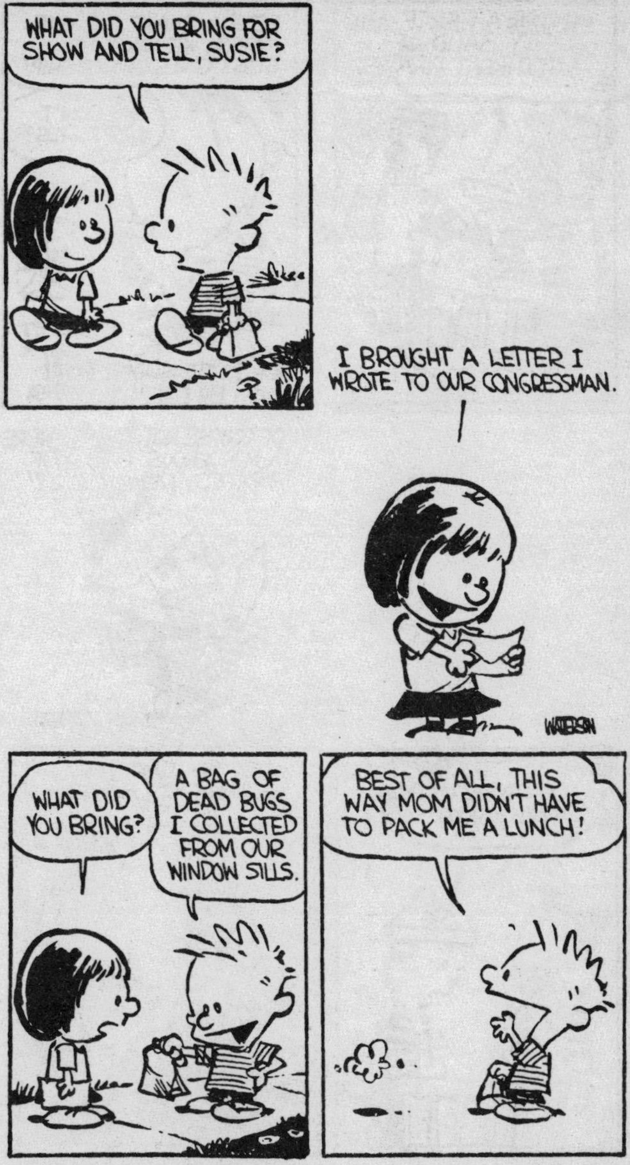
WHAT DID YOU BRING FOR SHOW AND TELL, SUSIE?
I BROUGHT A LETTER I WROTE TO OUR CONGRESSMAN.
WHAT DID YOU BRING?
A BAG OF DEAD BUGS I COLLECTED FROM OUR WINDOW SILLS.
BEST OF ALL, THIS WAY MOM DIDN'T HAVE TO PACK ME A LUNCH!

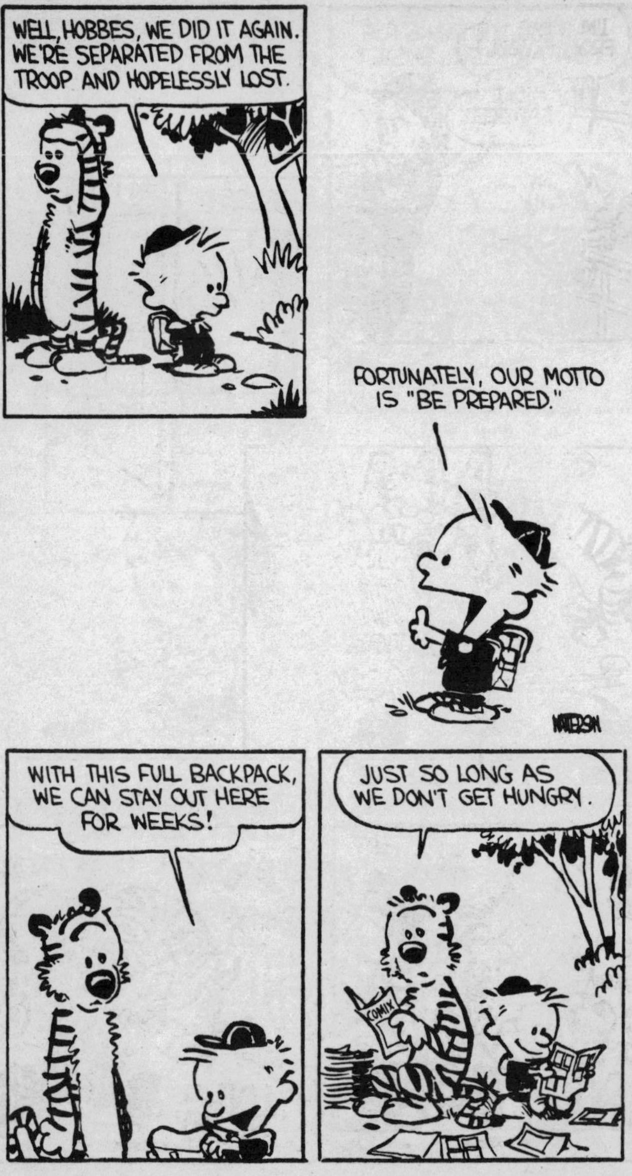

WELL, HOBBES, WE DID IT AGAIN. WE'RE SEPARATED FROM THE TROOP AND HOPELESSLY LOST.
FORTUNATELY, OUR MOTTO IS "BE PREPARED."
WATTERSON
WITH THIS FULL BACKPACK, WE CAN STAY OUT HERE FOR WEEKS!
JUST SO LONG AS WE DON'T GET HUNGRY.
COMIX

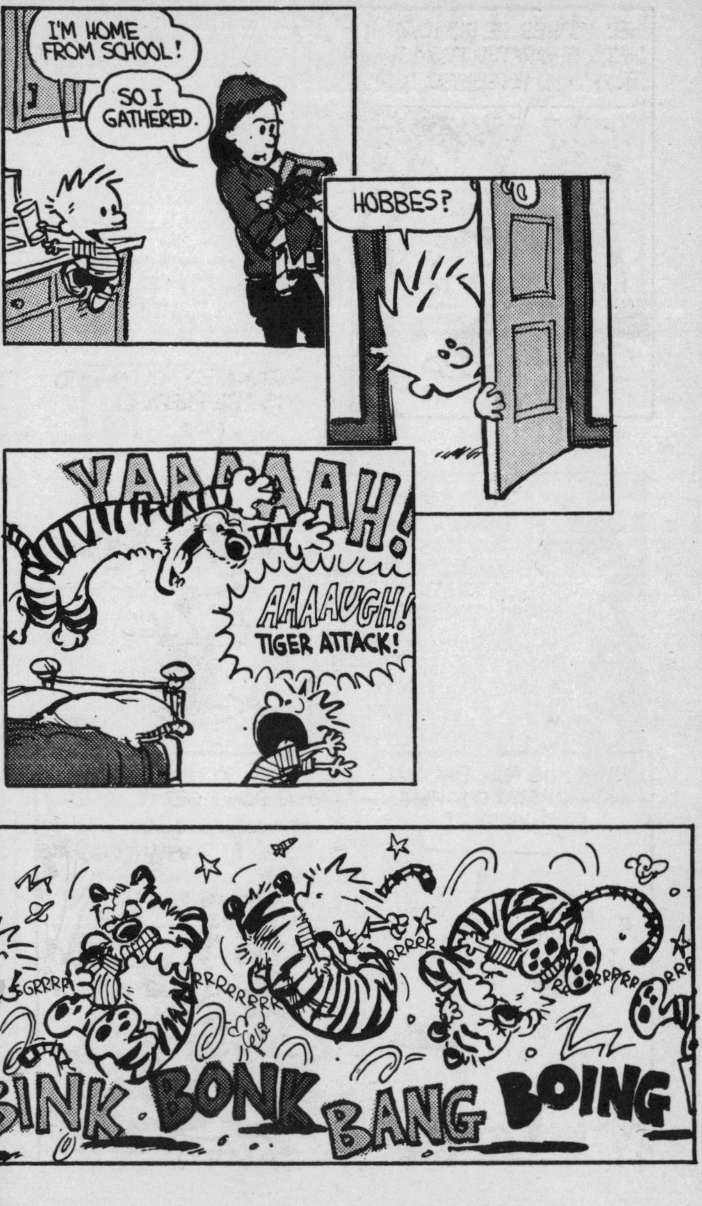
I'M HOME FROM SCHOOL!
SO I GATHERED.
HOBBES?
YAAAAAH!
AAAAUGH! TIGER ATTACK!
GRRRR
RRRRRRRRR
RRRRR
BINK
BONK
BANG
BOING

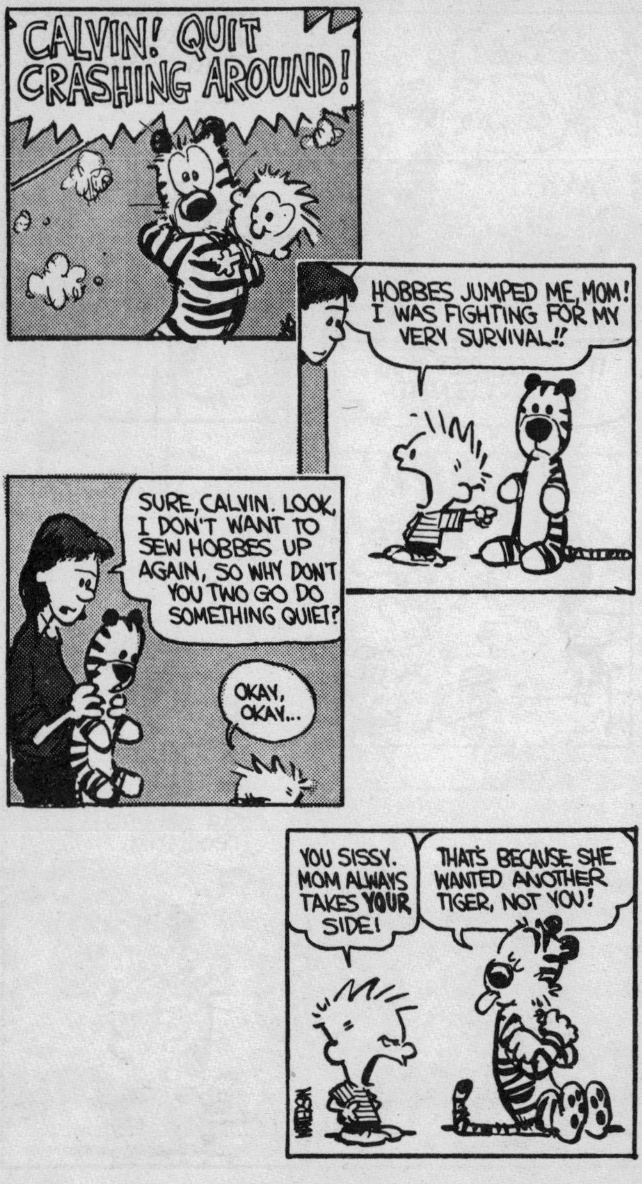
CALVIN! QUIT CRASHING AROUND!
HOBBES JUMPED ME, MOM! I WAS FIGHTING FOR MY VERY SURVIVAL!!
SURE, CALVIN. LOOK, I DON'T WANT TO SEW HOBBES UP AGAIN, SO WHY DON'T YOU TWO GO DO SOMETHING QUIET?
OKAY, OKAY...
YOU SISSY. MOM ALWAYS TAKES **YOUR** SIDE!
THAT'S BECAUSE SHE WANTED ANOTHER TIGER, NOT YOU!

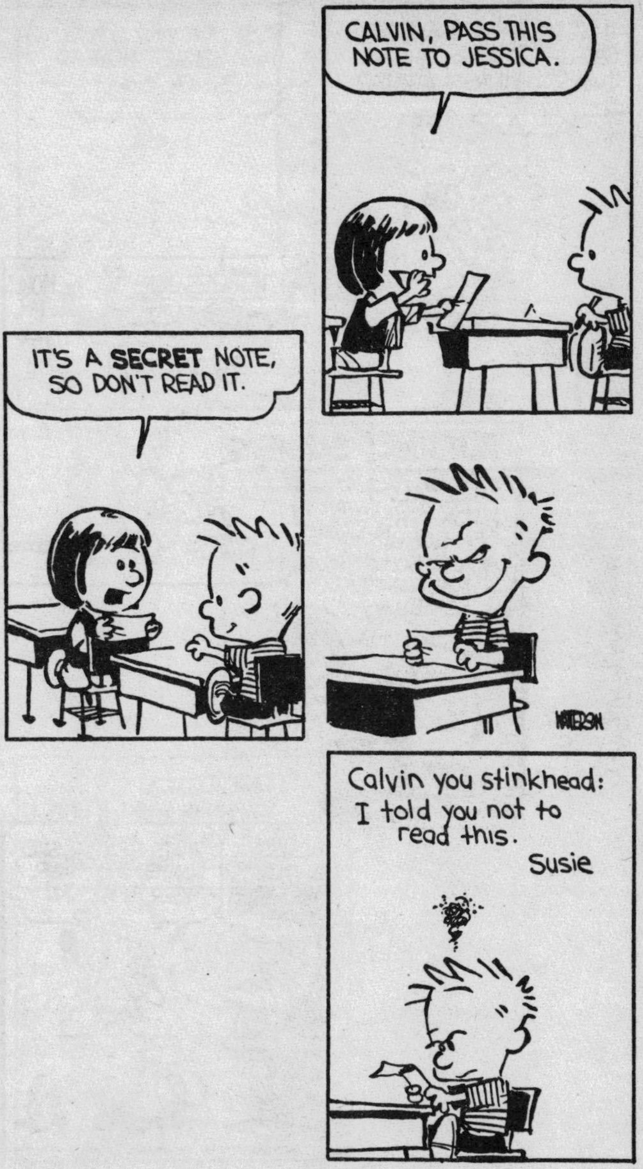
CALVIN, PASS THIS NOTE TO JESSICA.
IT'S A **SECRET** NOTE, SO DON'T READ IT.
Calvin you stinkhead:
I told you not to read this.
Susie

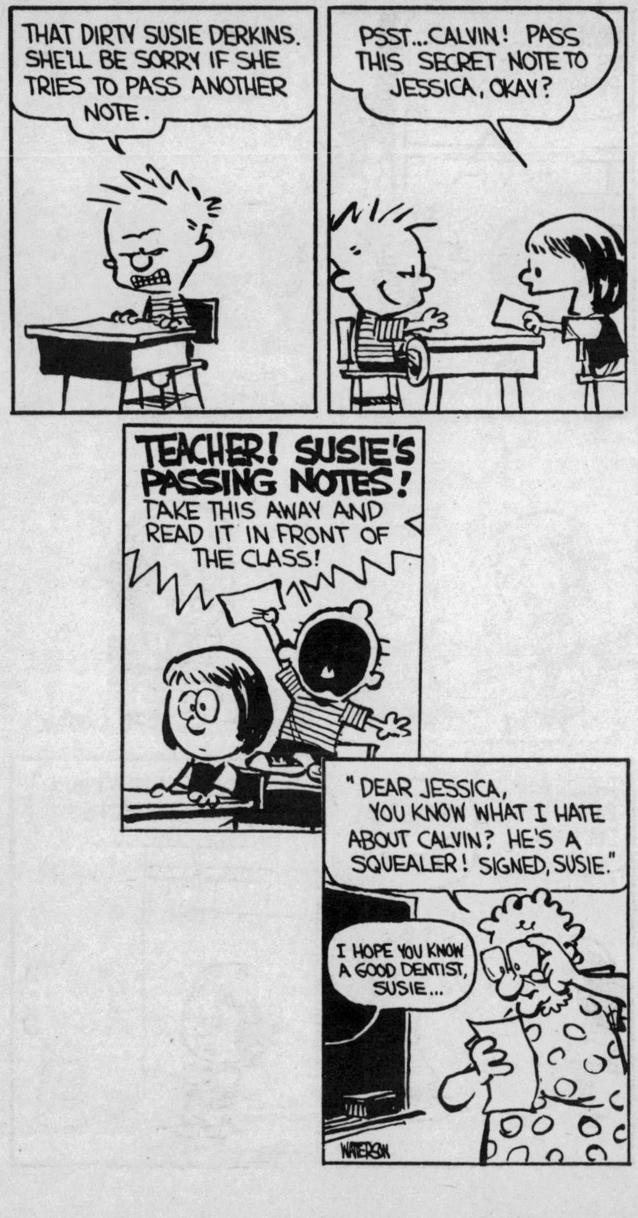
THAT DIRTY SUSIE DERKINS. SHE'LL BE SORRY IF SHE TRIES TO PASS ANOTHER NOTE.
PSST...CALVIN! PASS THIS SECRET NOTE TO JESSICA, OKAY?
TEACHER! SUSIE'S PASSING NOTES! TAKE THIS AWAY AND READ IT IN FRONT OF THE CLASS!
"DEAR JESSICA, YOU KNOW WHAT I HATE ABOUT CALVIN? HE'S A SQUEALER! SIGNED, SUSIE."
I HOPE YOU KNOW A GOOD DENTIST, SUSIE...
WATERSON

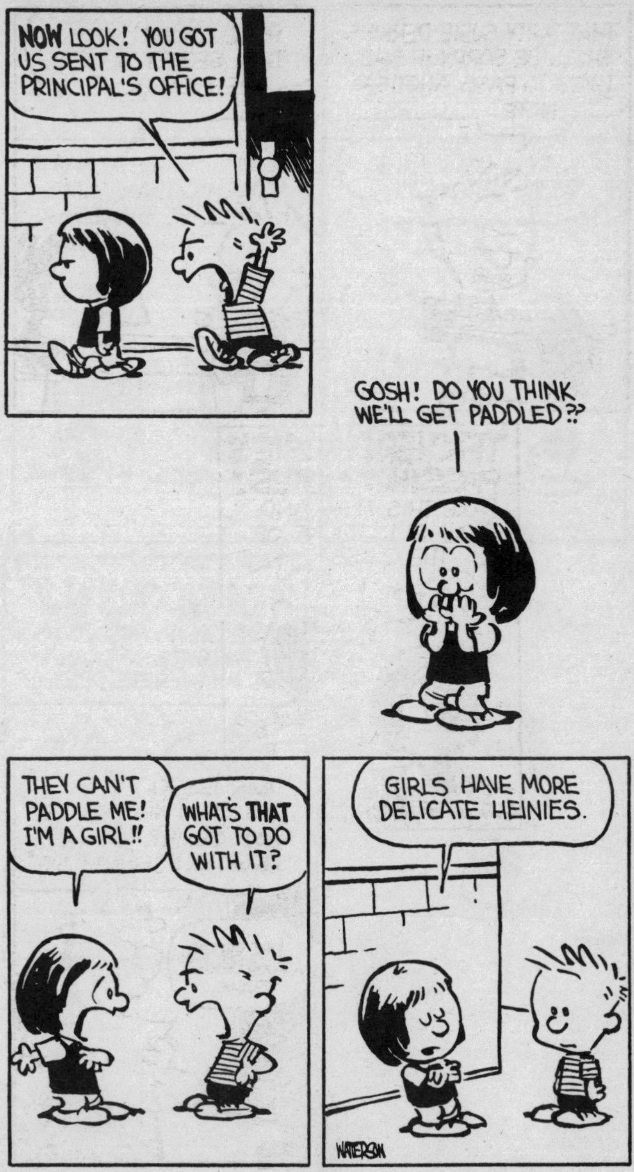
NOW LOOK! YOU GOT US SENT TO THE PRINCIPAL'S OFFICE!
GOSH! DO YOU THINK WE'LL GET PADDLED??
THEY CAN'T PADDLE ME! I'M A GIRL!!
WHAT'S THAT GOT TO DO WITH IT?
GIRLS HAVE MORE DELICATE HEINIES.
WATERSON

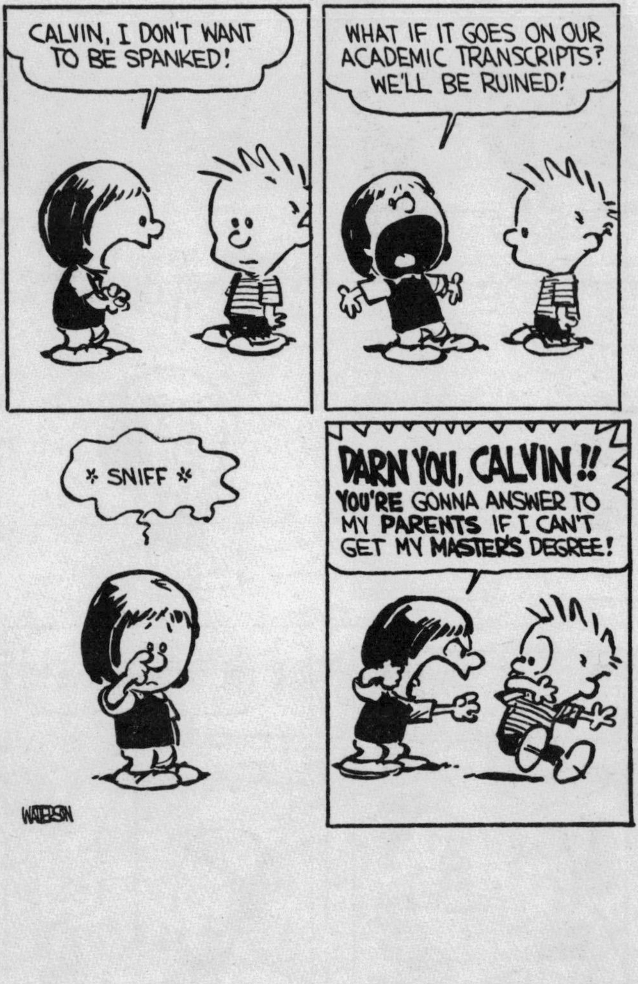
CALVIN, I DON'T WANT TO BE SPANKED!
WHAT IF IT GOES ON OUR ACADEMIC TRANSCRIPTS? WE'LL BE RUINED!
* SNIFF *
DARN YOU, CALVIN!! YOU'RE GONNA ANSWER TO MY PARENTS IF I CAN'T GET MY MASTER'S DEGREE!
WATTERSON

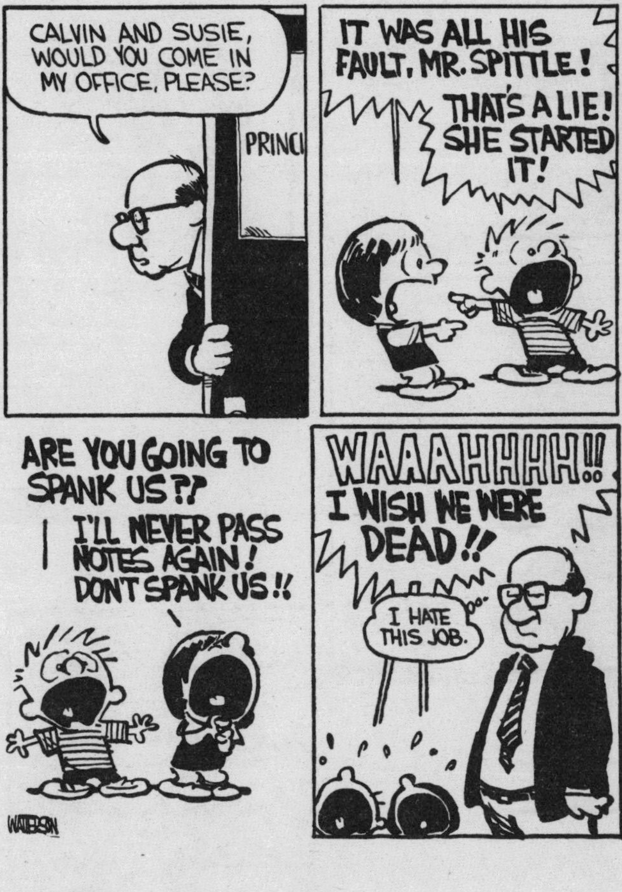
CALVIN AND SUSIE, WOULD YOU COME IN MY OFFICE, PLEASE?
PRINCI
IT WAS ALL HIS FAULT, MR. SPITTLE!
THAT'S A LIE! SHE STARTED IT!
ARE YOU GOING TO SPANK US?!
I'LL NEVER PASS NOTES AGAIN! DON'T SPANK US!!
WATTERSON
WAAAHHHH!!
I WISH WE WERE DEAD!!
I HATE THIS JOB.

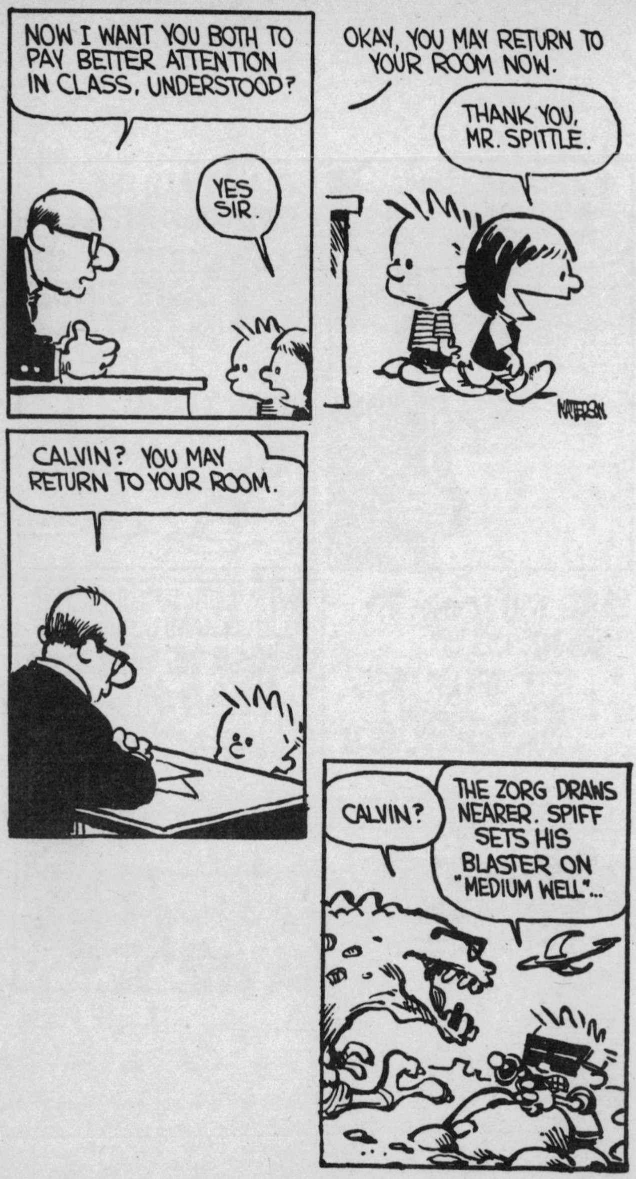
NOW I WANT YOU BOTH TO PAY BETTER ATTENTION IN CLASS, UNDERSTOOD?
YES SIR.
OKAY, YOU MAY RETURN TO YOUR ROOM NOW.
THANK YOU, MR. SPITTLE.
CALVIN? YOU MAY RETURN TO YOUR ROOM.
CALVIN?
THE ZORG DRAWS NEARER. SPIFF SETS HIS BLASTER ON "MEDIUM WELL"...

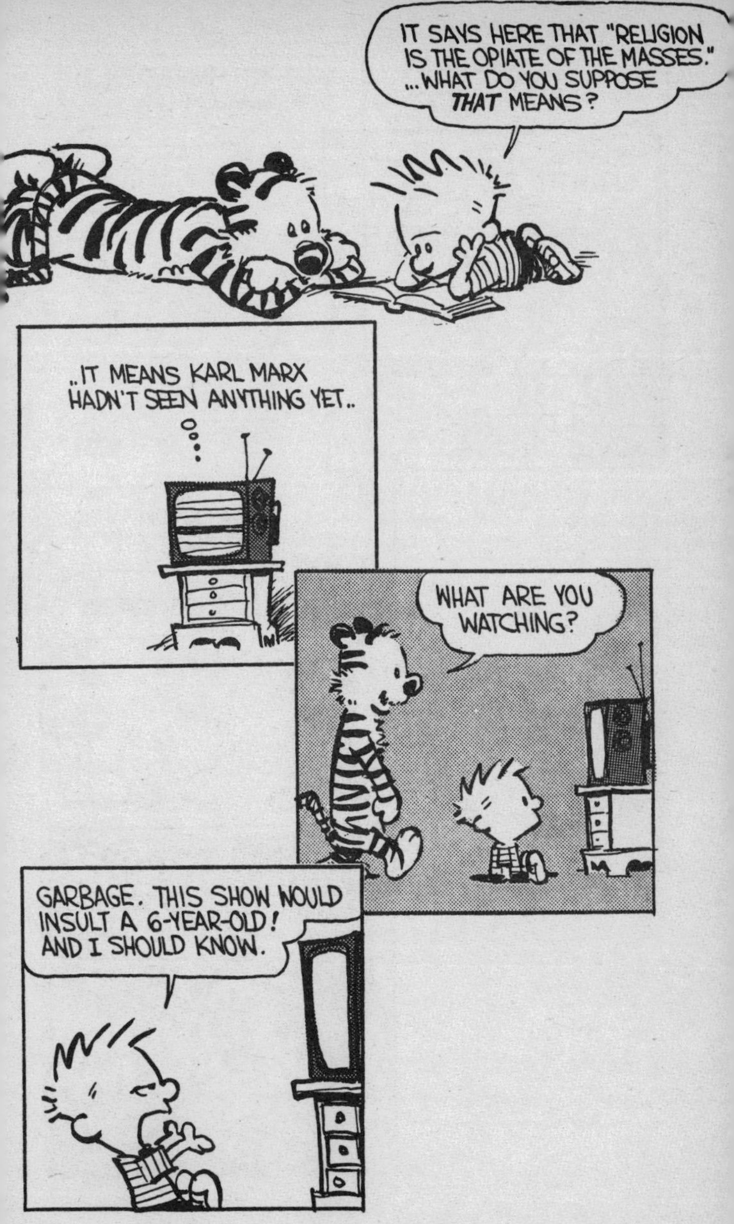
IT SAYS HERE THAT "RELIGION IS THE OPIATE OF THE MASSES." ...WHAT DO YOU SUPPOSE THAT MEANS?
..IT MEANS KARL MARX HADN'T SEEN ANYTHING YET..
WHAT ARE YOU WATCHING?
GARBAGE. THIS SHOW WOULD INSULT A 6-YEAR-OLD! AND I SHOULD KNOW.

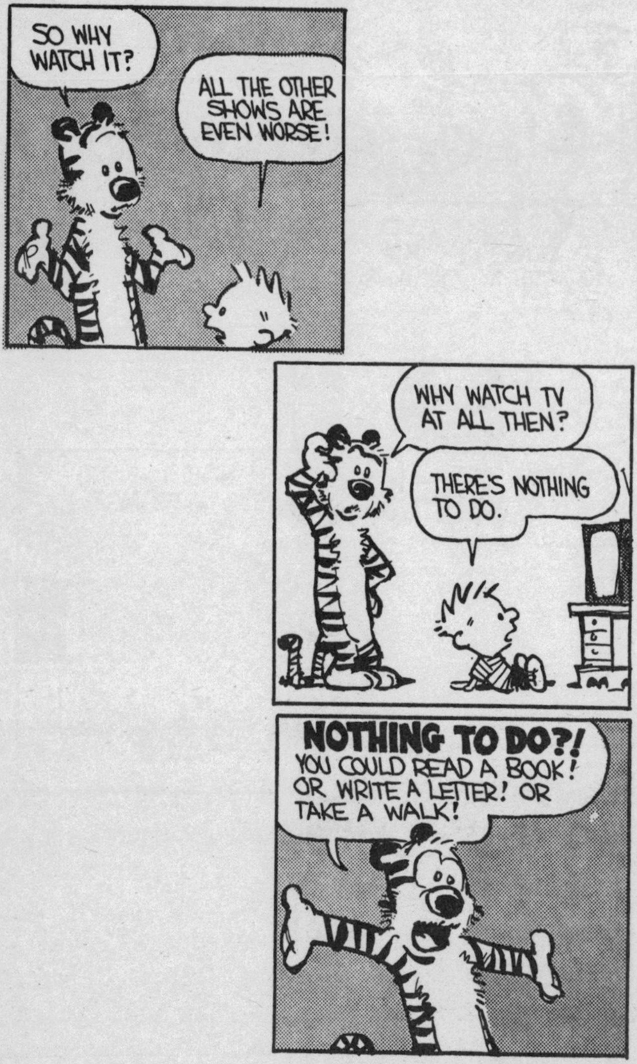
SO WHY WATCH IT?
ALL THE OTHER SHOWS ARE EVEN WORSE!
WHY WATCH TV AT ALL THEN?
THERE'S NOTHING TO DO.
NOTHING TO DO?! YOU COULD READ A BOOK! OR WRITE A LETTER! OR TAKE A WALK!

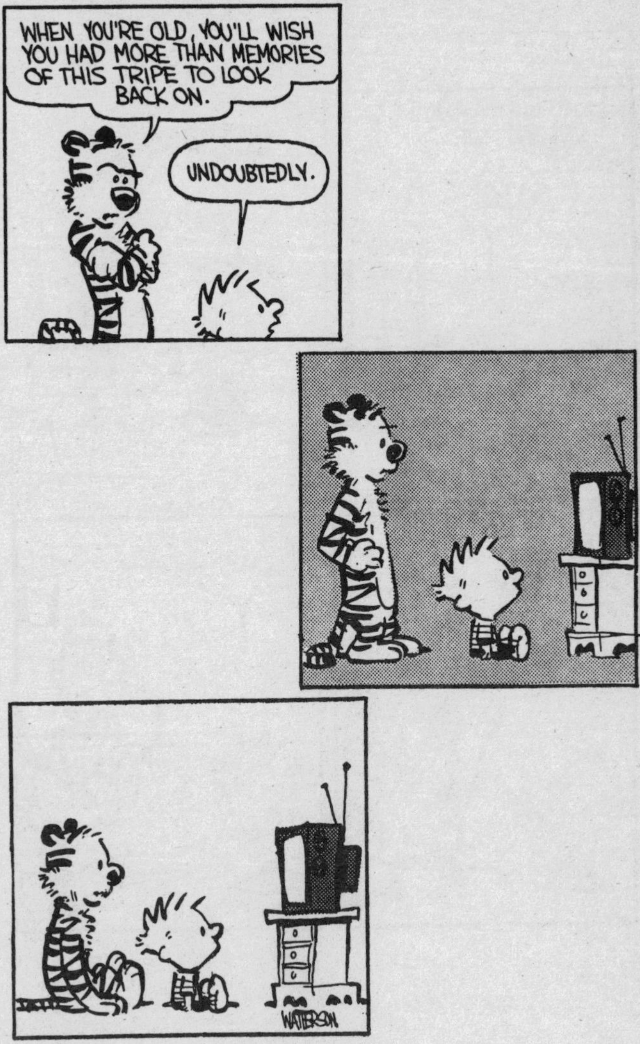
WHEN YOU'RE OLD, YOU'LL WISH YOU HAD MORE THAN MEMORIES OF THIS TRIPE TO LOOK BACK ON.
UNDOUBTEDLY.
WATTERSON

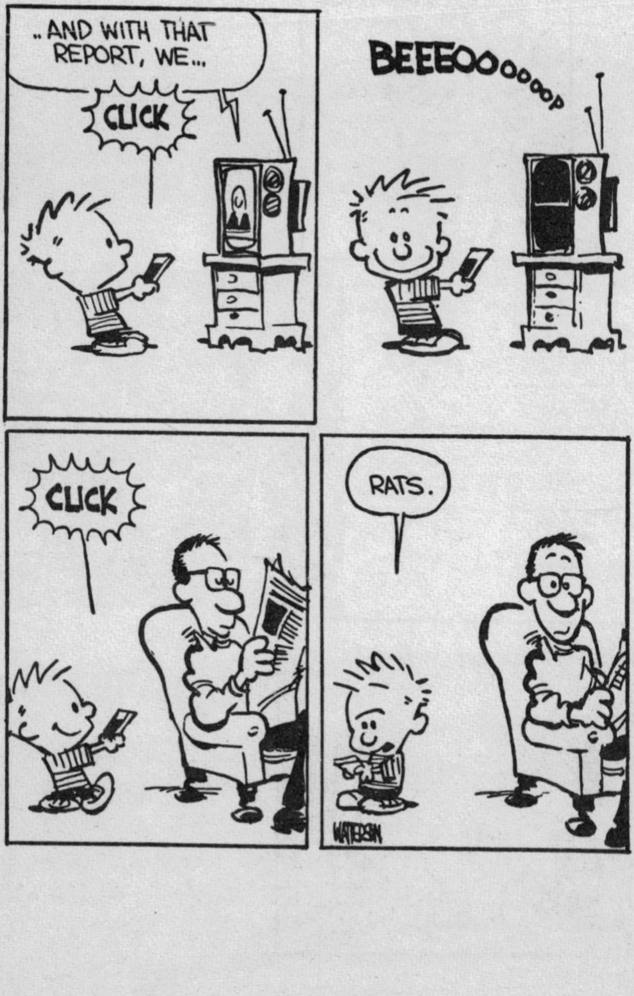
..AND WITH THAT REPORT, WE...
CLICK
BEEEOOooooop
CLICK
RATS.
WATTERSON

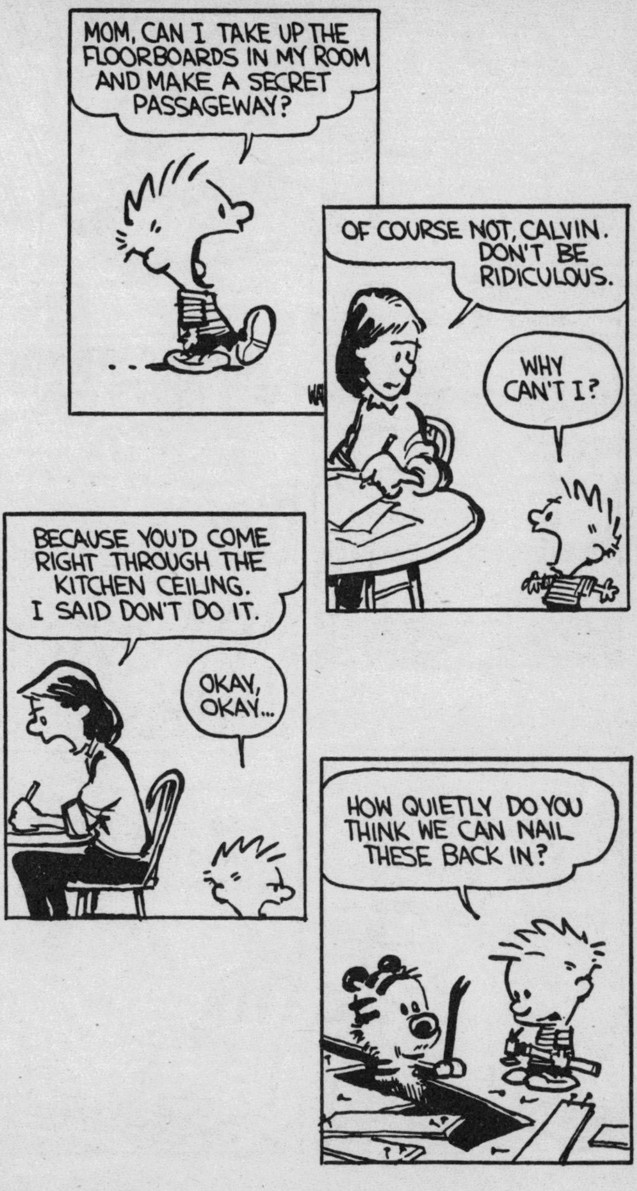

MOM, CAN I TAKE UP THE FLOORBOARDS IN MY ROOM AND MAKE A SECRET PASSAGEWAY?
OF COURSE NOT, CALVIN. DON'T BE RIDICULOUS.
WHY CAN'T I?
BECAUSE YOU'D COME RIGHT THROUGH THE KITCHEN CEILING. I SAID DON'T DO IT.
OKAY, OKAY...
HOW QUIETLY DO YOU THINK WE CAN NAIL THESE BACK IN?

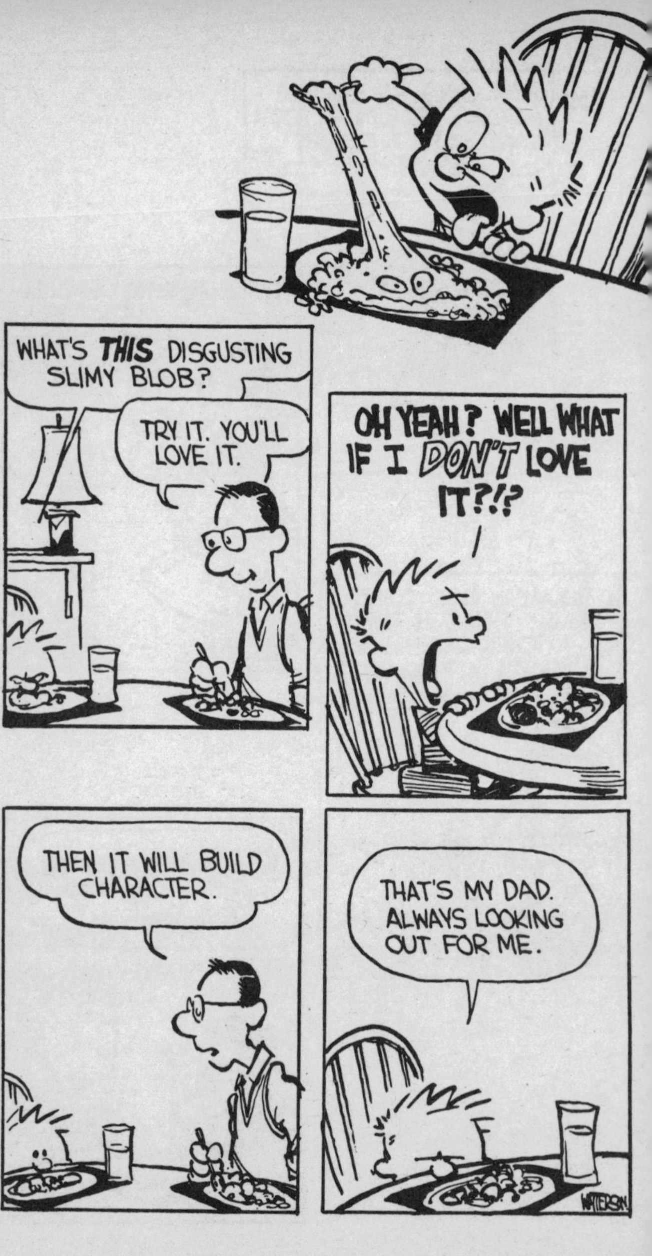
WHAT'S THIS DISGUSTING SLIMY BLOB?
TRY IT. YOU'LL LOVE IT.
OH YEAH? WELL WHAT IF I DON'T LOVE IT?!?
THEN IT WILL BUILD CHARACTER.
THAT'S MY DAD. ALWAYS LOOKING OUT FOR ME.
WATTERSON

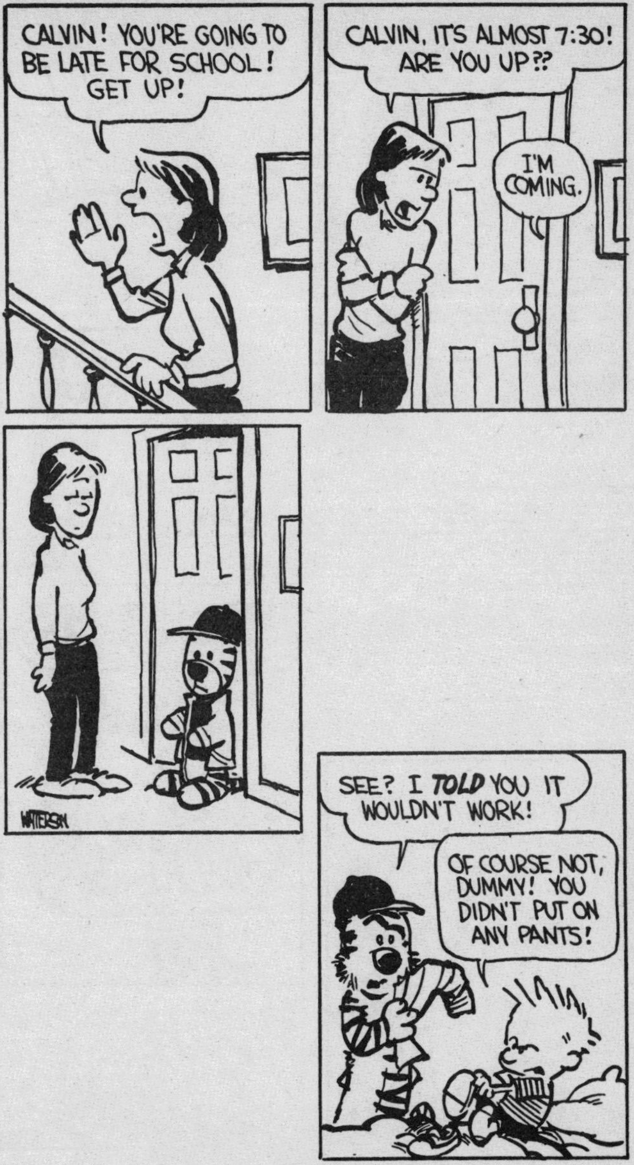
CALVIN! YOU'RE GOING TO BE LATE FOR SCHOOL! GET UP!
CALVIN, IT'S ALMOST 7:30! ARE YOU UP??
I'M COMING.
WATTERSON
SEE? I TOLD YOU IT WOULDN'T WORK!
OF COURSE NOT, DUMMY! YOU DIDN'T PUT ON ANY PANTS!

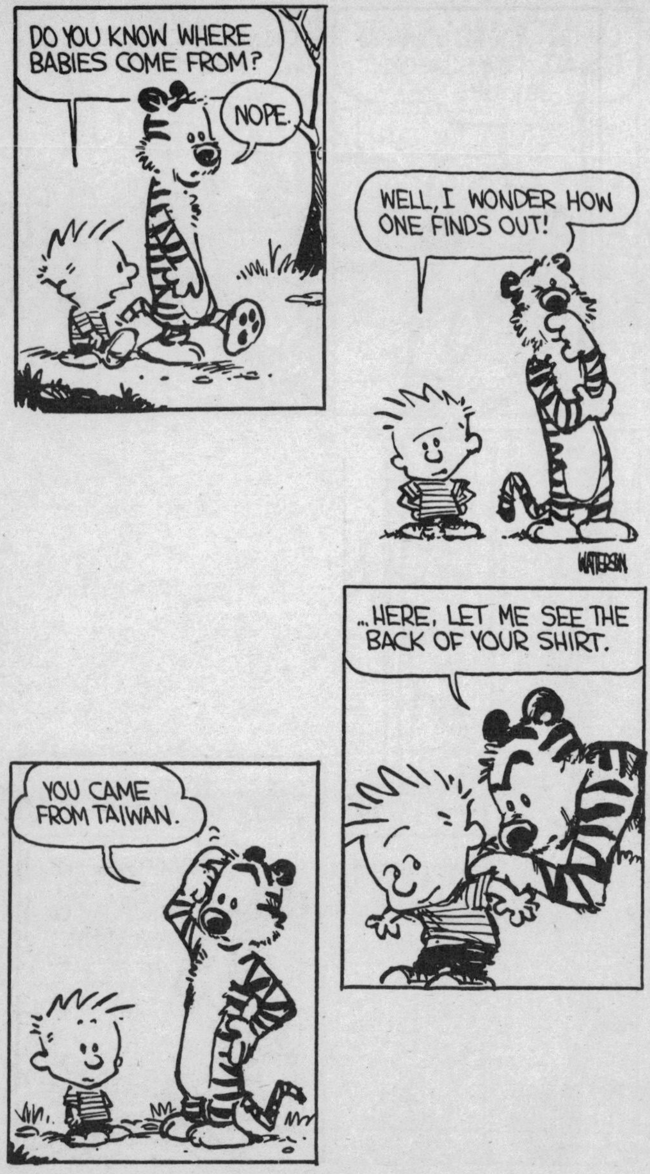
DO YOU KNOW WHERE BABIES COME FROM?
NOPE.
...HERE, LET ME SEE THE BACK OF YOUR SHIRT.
YOU CAME FROM TAIWAN.
WELL, I WONDER HOW ONE FINDS OUT!
WATTERSON

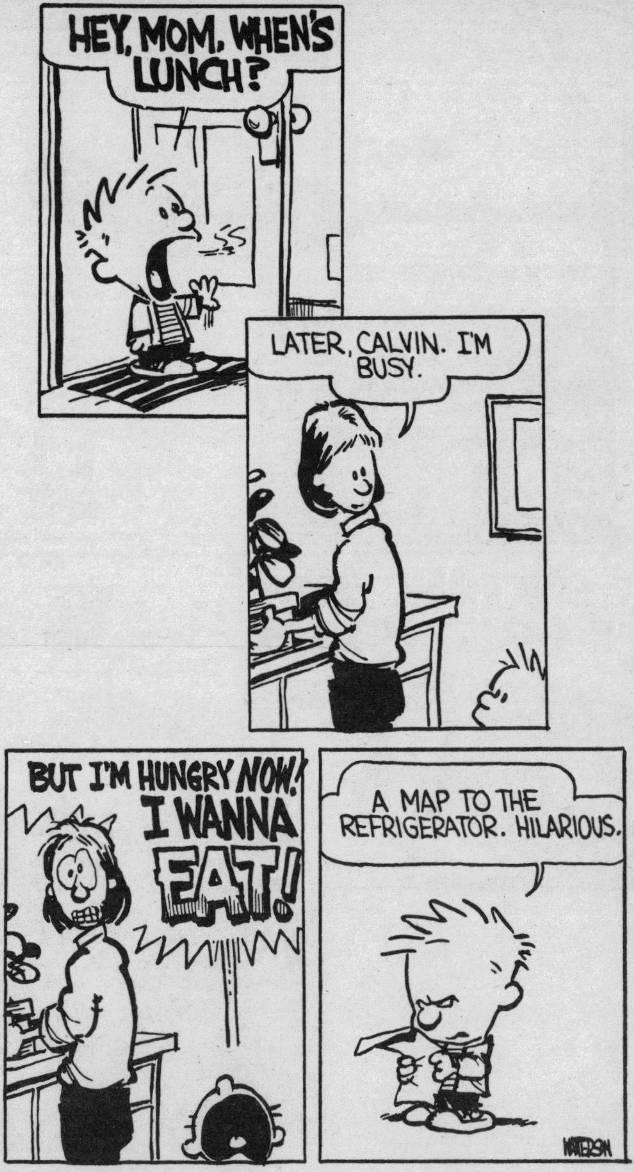
HEY, MOM, WHEN'S LUNCH?
LATER, CALVIN. I'M BUSY.
BUT I'M HUNGRY NOW! I WANNA EAT!
A MAP TO THE REFRIGERATOR. HILARIOUS.
WATTERSON

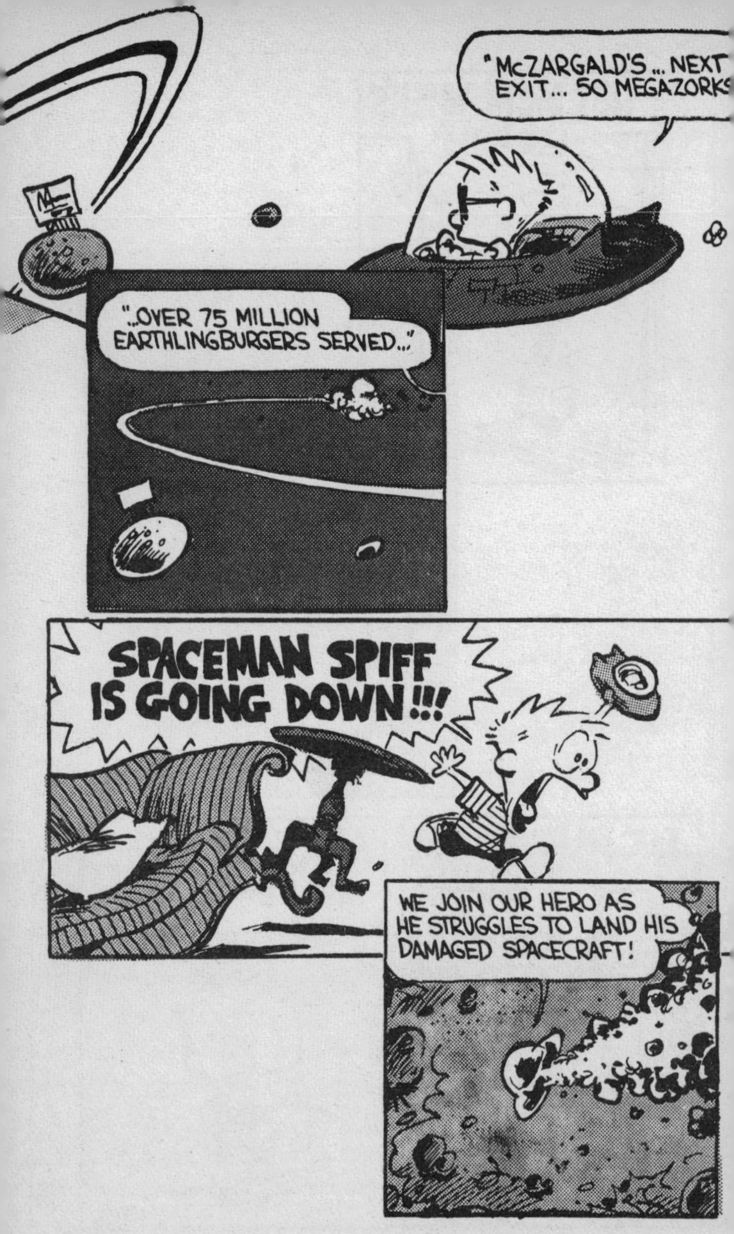

"McZARGALD'S ... NEXT EXIT... 50 MEGAZORKS
"...OVER 75 MILLION EARTHLINGBURGERS SERVED..."
SPACEMAN SPIFF IS GOING DOWN!!!
WE JOIN OUR HERO AS HE STRUGGLES TO LAND HIS DAMAGED SPACECRAFT!

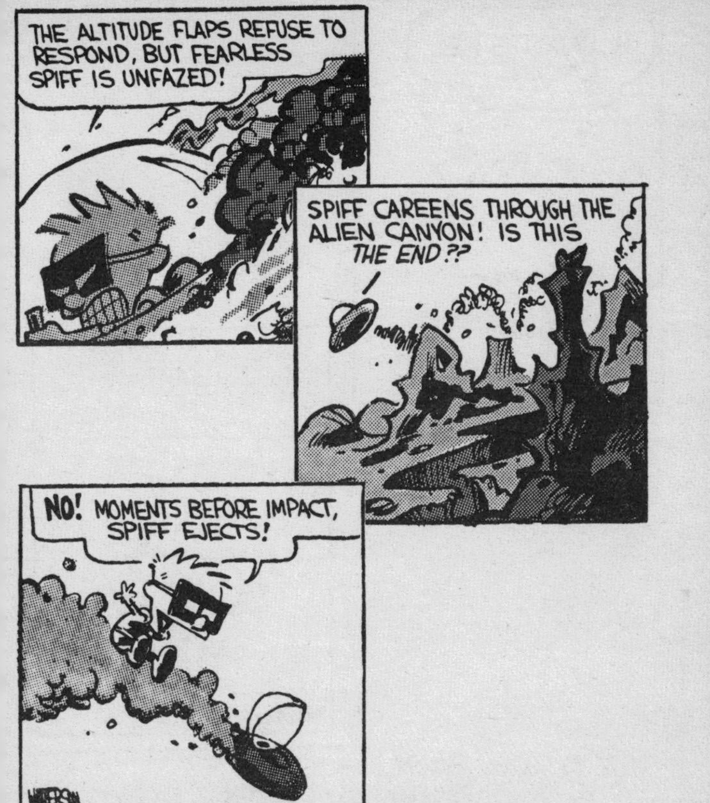
THE ALTITUDE FLAPS REFUSE TO RESPOND, BUT FEARLESS SPIFF IS UNFAZED!
SPIFF CAREENS THROUGH THE ALIEN CANYON! IS THIS *THE END??*
NO! MOMENTS BEFORE IMPACT, SPIFF EJECTS!
WATERSON
NOW ARE YOU THROUGH CHARGING AROUND THE HOUSE, OR ARE YOU GOING TO FALL DOWN THE STAIRS AGAIN?
OUR HERO REGAINS CONSCIOUSNESS AT THE FEET OF A SARCASTIC ALIEN...

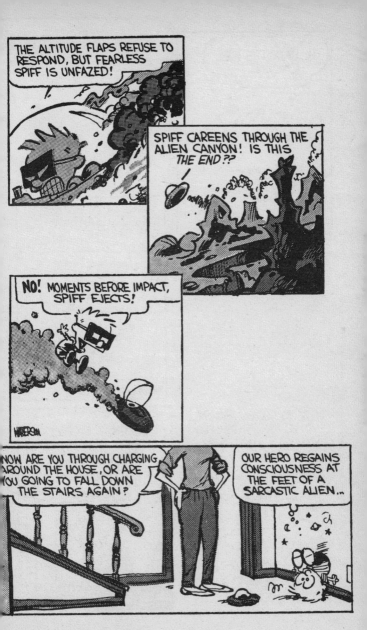

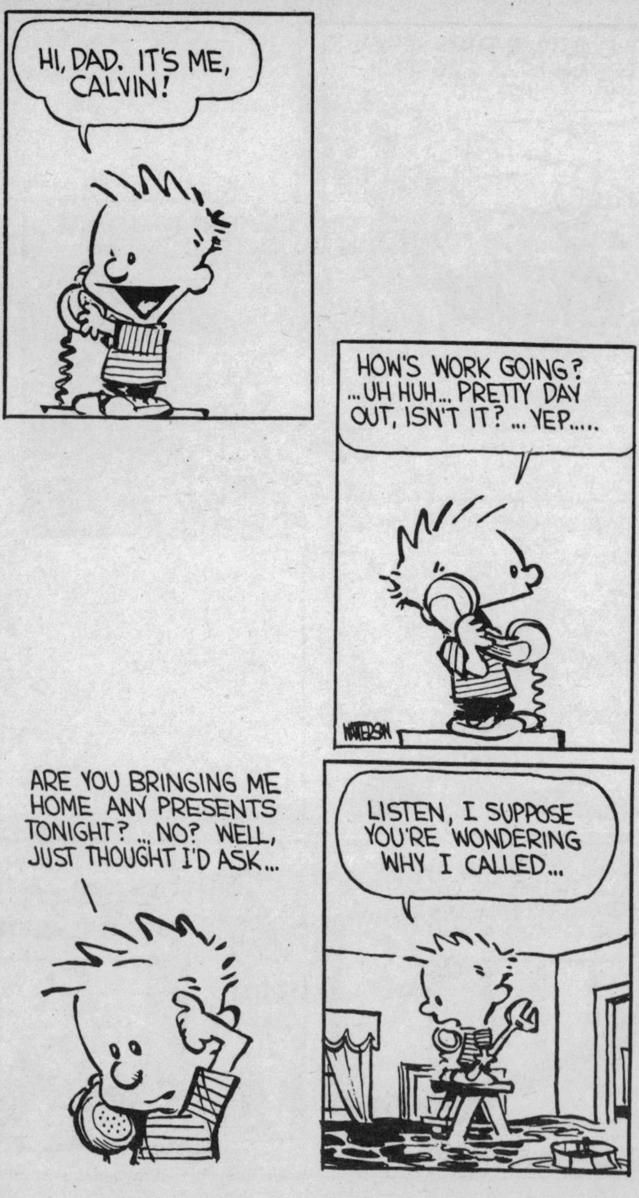

HI, DAD. IT'S ME, CALVIN!
HOW'S WORK GOING? ...UH HUH... PRETTY DAY OUT, ISN'T IT? ... YEP.....
WATTERSON
LISTEN, I SUPPOSE YOU'RE WONDERING WHY I CALLED...
ARE YOU BRINGING ME HOME ANY PRESENTS TONIGHT? ... NO? WELL, JUST THOUGHT I'D ASK...

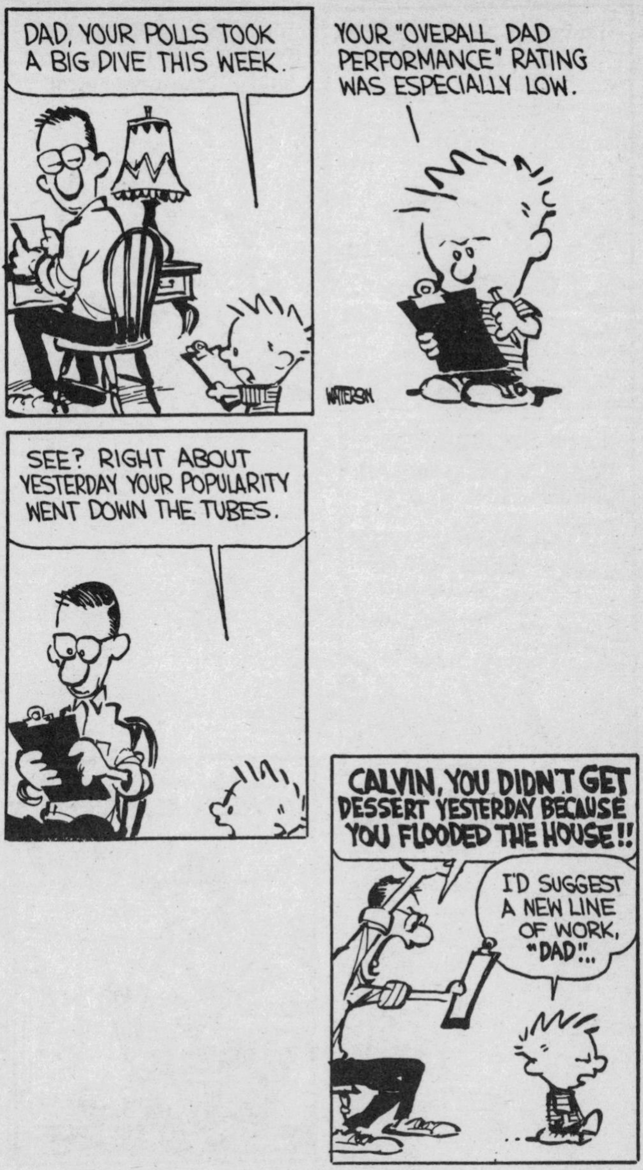
DAD, YOUR POLLS TOOK A BIG DIVE THIS WEEK.
YOUR "OVERALL DAD PERFORMANCE" RATING WAS ESPECIALLY LOW.
WATTERSON
SEE? RIGHT ABOUT YESTERDAY YOUR POPULARITY WENT DOWN THE TUBES.
CALVIN, YOU DIDN'T GET DESSERT YESTERDAY BECAUSE YOU FLOODED THE HOUSE!!
I'D SUGGEST A NEW LINE OF WORK, "DAD"...

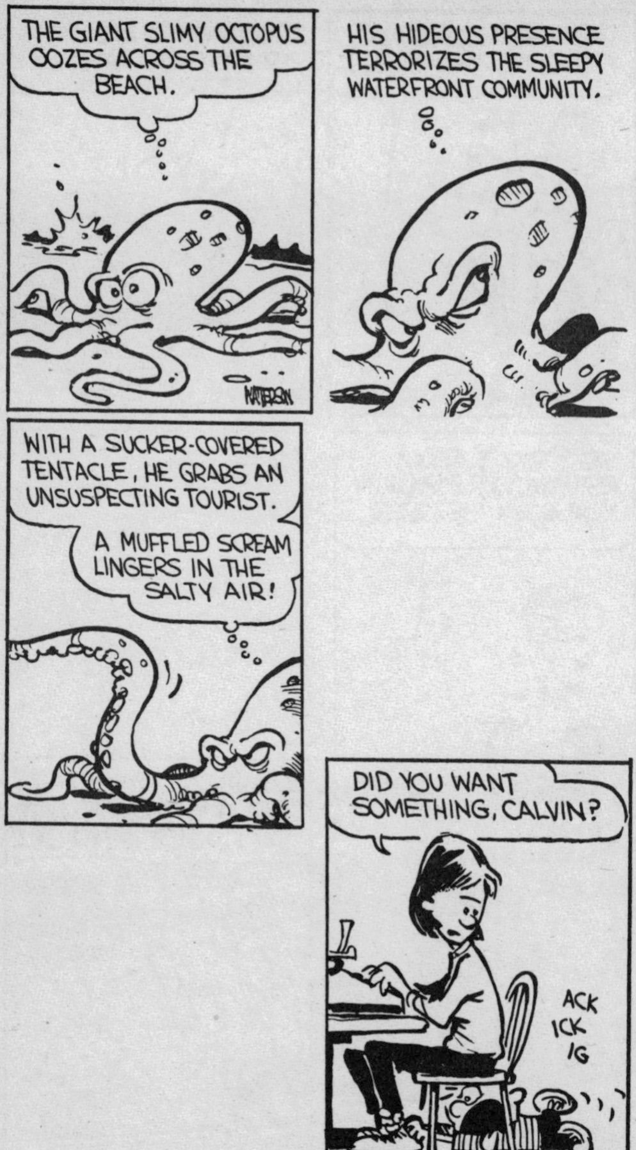
THE GIANT SLIMY OCTOPUS OOZES ACROSS THE BEACH.
HIS HIDEOUS PRESENCE TERRORIZES THE SLEEPY WATERFRONT COMMUNITY.
WITH A SUCKER-COVERED TENTACLE, HE GRABS AN UNSUSPECTING TOURIST.
A MUFFLED SCREAM LINGERS IN THE SALTY AIR!
DID YOU WANT SOMETHING, CALVIN?
ACK
ICK
IG

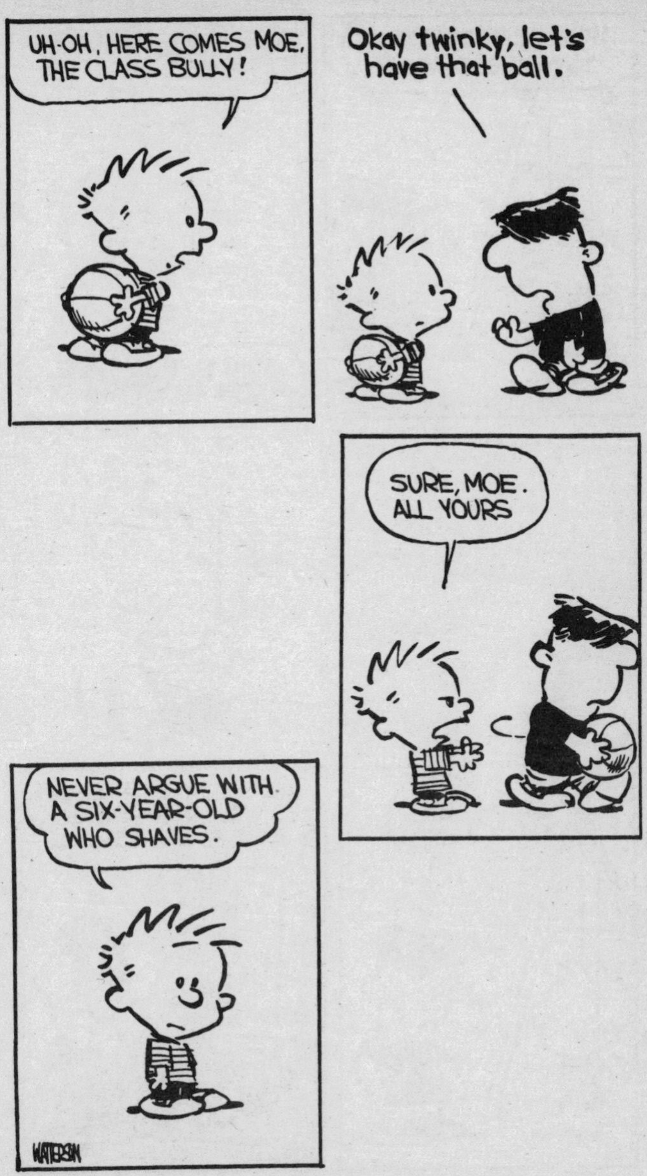
UH-OH, HERE COMES MOE, THE CLASS BULLY!
Okay twinky, let's have that ball.
SURE, MOE. ALL YOURS
NEVER ARGUE WITH A SIX-YEAR-OLD WHO SHAVES.
WATERSON

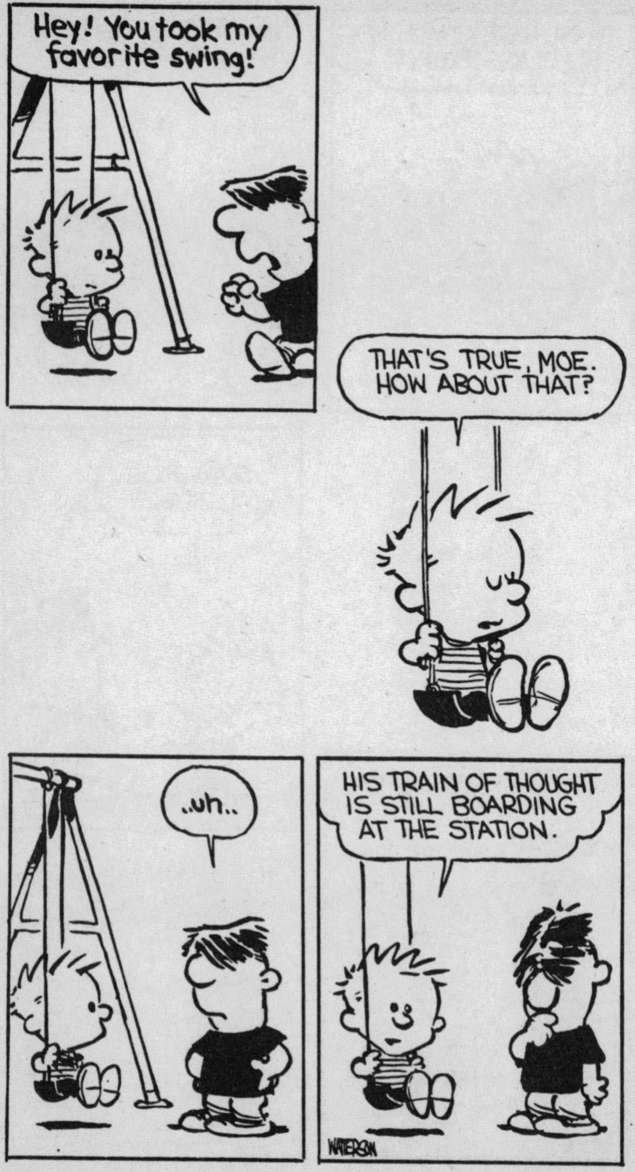
Hey! You took my favorite swing!
THAT'S TRUE, MOE. HOW ABOUT THAT?
..uh..
HIS TRAIN OF THOUGHT IS STILL BOARDING AT THE STATION.
WATERSON

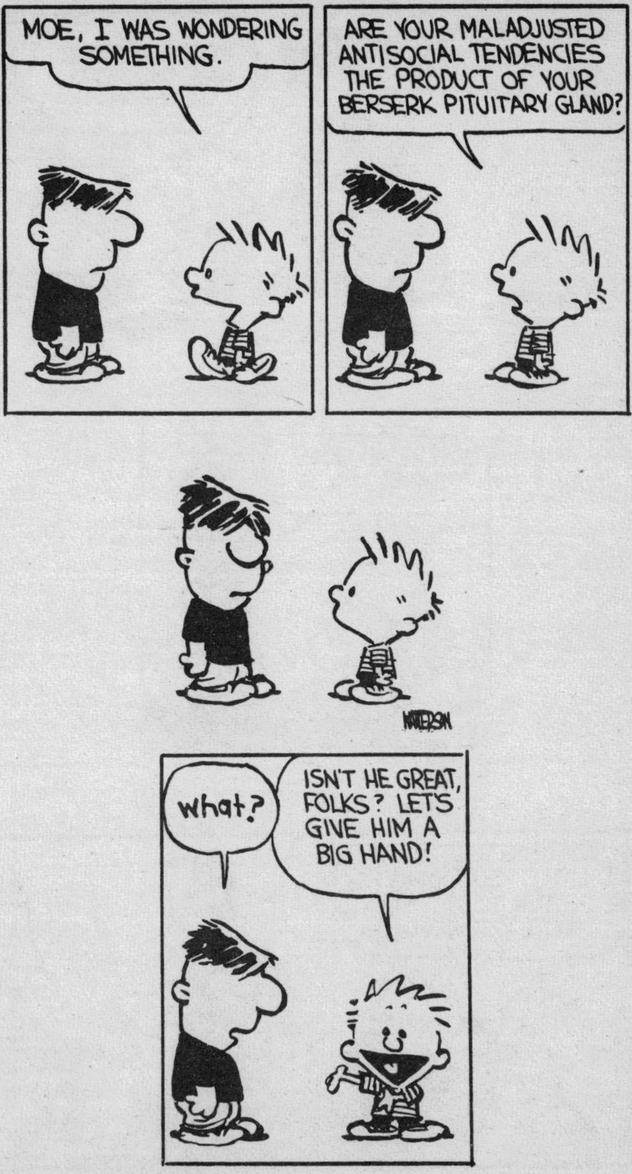
MOE, I WAS WONDERING SOMETHING.
ARE YOUR MALADJUSTED ANTISOCIAL TENDENCIES THE PRODUCT OF YOUR BERSERK PITUITARY GLAND?
what?
ISN'T HE GREAT, FOLKS? LET'S GIVE HIM A BIG HAND!

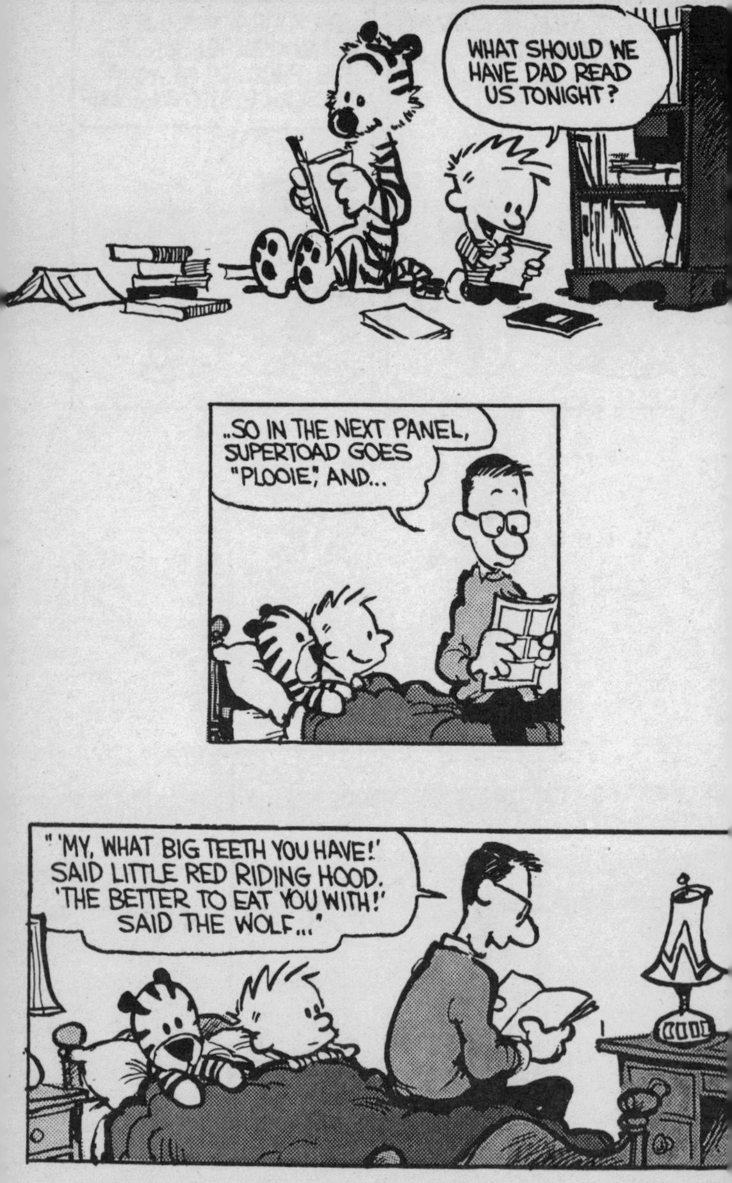
WHAT SHOULD WE HAVE DAD READ US TONIGHT?
..SO IN THE NEXT PANEL, SUPERTOAD GOES "PLOOIE," AND...
" 'MY, WHAT BIG TEETH YOU HAVE!' SAID LITTLE RED RIDING HOOD. 'THE BETTER TO EAT YOU WITH!' SAID THE WOLF..."

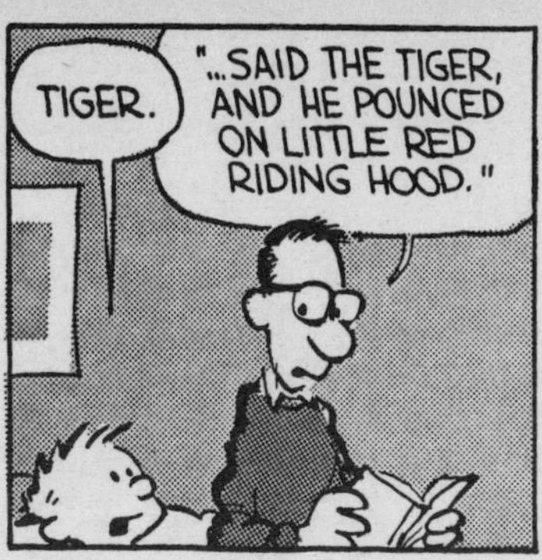
TIGER.
"...SAID THE TIGER, AND HE POUNCED ON LITTLE RED RIDING HOOD."

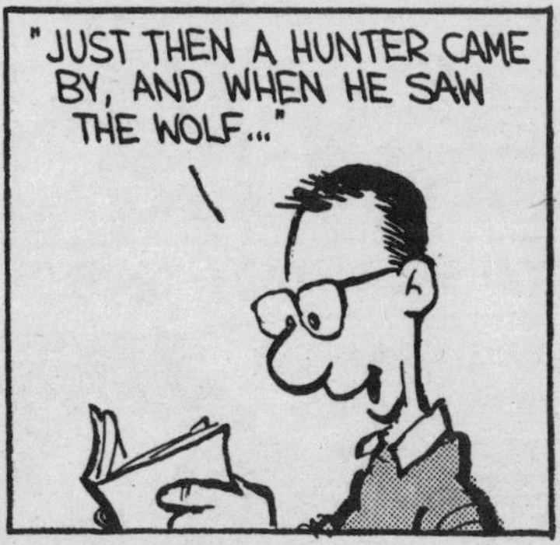
"JUST THEN A HUNTER CAME BY, AND WHEN HE SAW THE WOLF..."

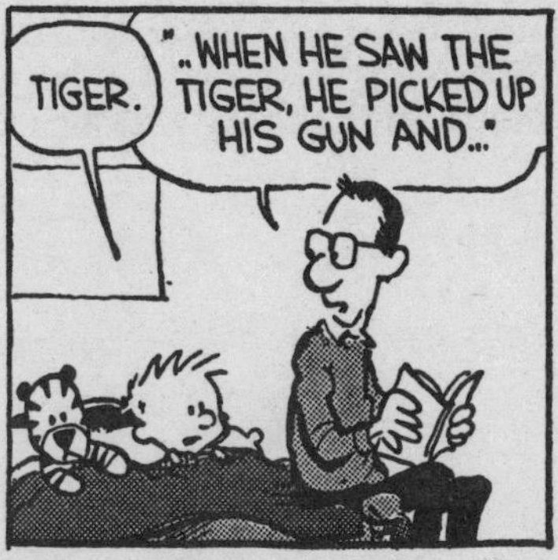
TIGER.
"..WHEN HE SAW THE TIGER, HE PICKED UP HIS GUN AND..."

..AND?
"...AND IT WAS TOO LATE. THE TIGER ATE THEM BOTH AND HE LIVED HAPPILY EVER AFTER. THE END."
GOOD STORY, DAD! THANKS!
SNIFF I ALWAYS CRY AT HAPPY ENDINGS.
WATTERSON

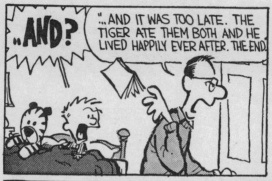

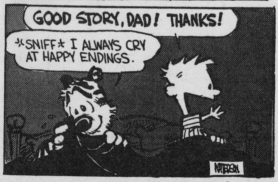

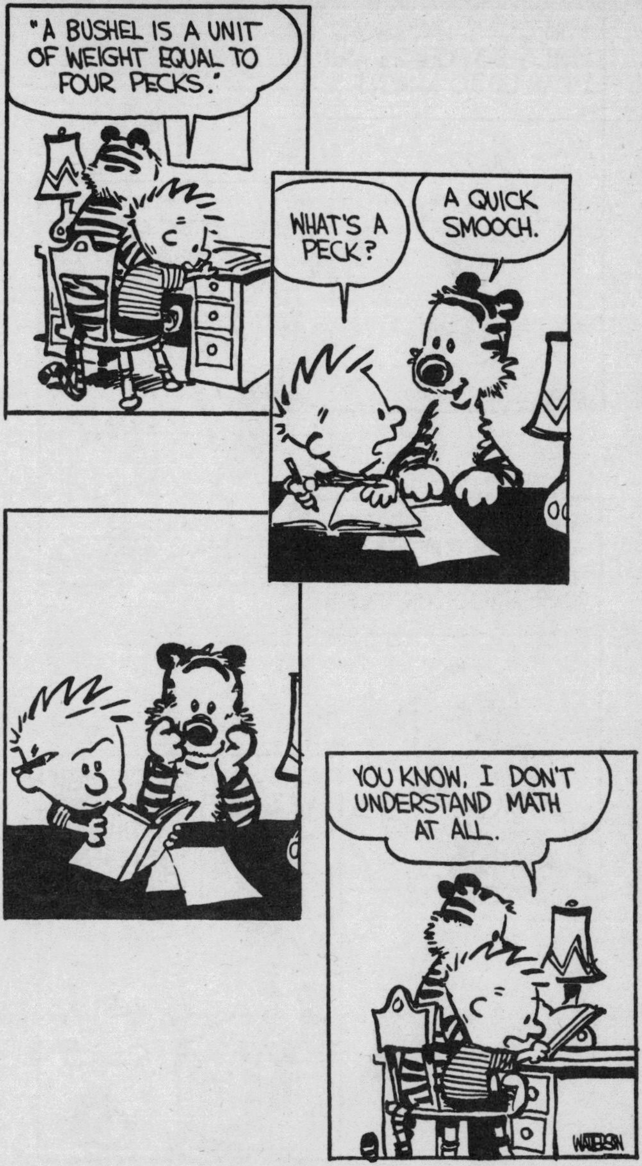
"A BUSHEL IS A UNIT OF WEIGHT EQUAL TO FOUR PECKS."
WHAT'S A PECK?
A QUICK SMOOCH.
YOU KNOW, I DON'T UNDERSTAND MATH AT ALL.
WATTERSON

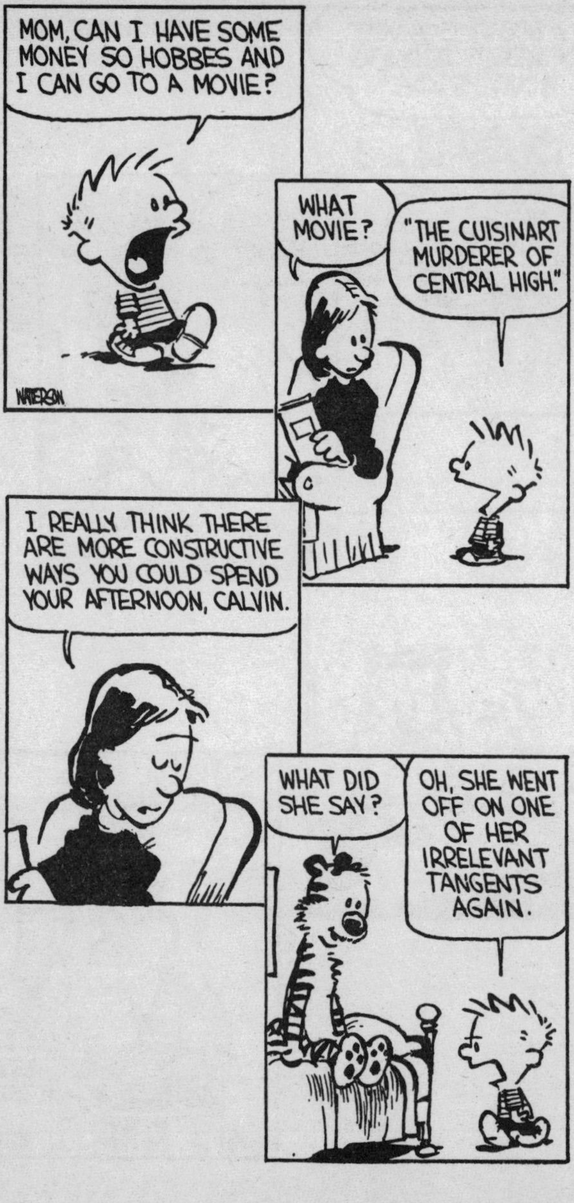
MOM, CAN I HAVE SOME MONEY SO HOBBES AND I CAN GO TO A MOVIE?
WATERSON
WHAT MOVIE?
"THE CUISINART MURDERER OF CENTRAL HIGH."
I REALLY THINK THERE ARE MORE CONSTRUCTIVE WAYS YOU COULD SPEND YOUR AFTERNOON, CALVIN.
WHAT DID SHE SAY?
OH, SHE WENT OFF ON ONE OF HER IRRELEVANT TANGENTS AGAIN.

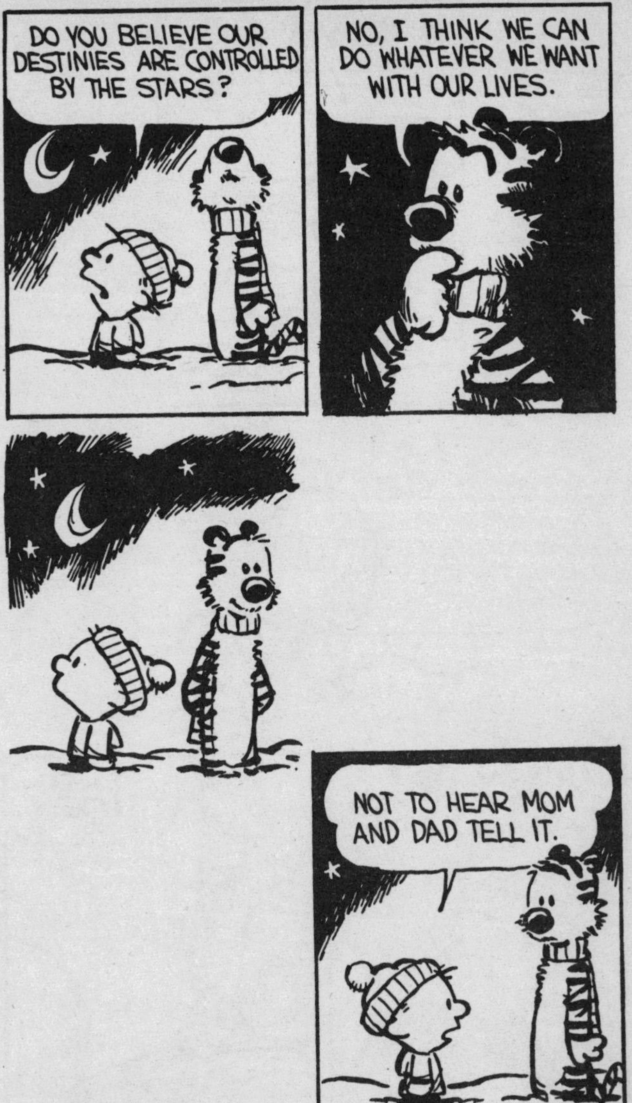
DO YOU BELIEVE OUR DESTINIES ARE CONTROLLED BY THE STARS?
NO, I THINK WE CAN DO WHATEVER WE WANT WITH OUR LIVES.
NOT TO HEAR MOM AND DAD TELL IT.
WATERSON

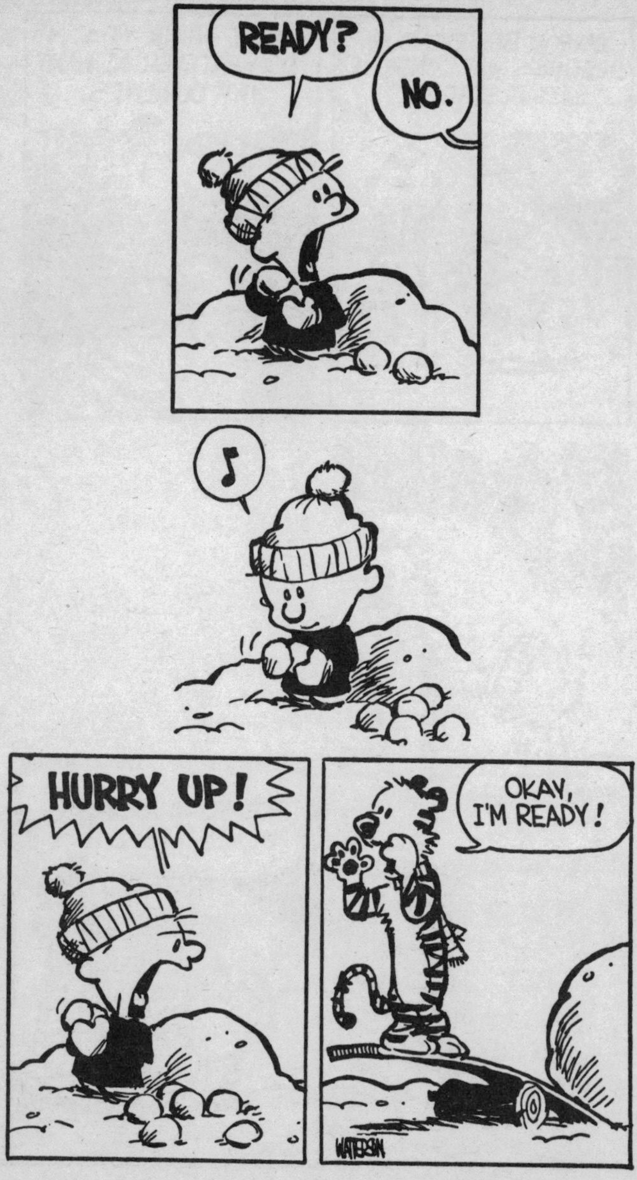
READY?
NO.
HURRY UP!
OKAY, I'M READY!
WATTERSON

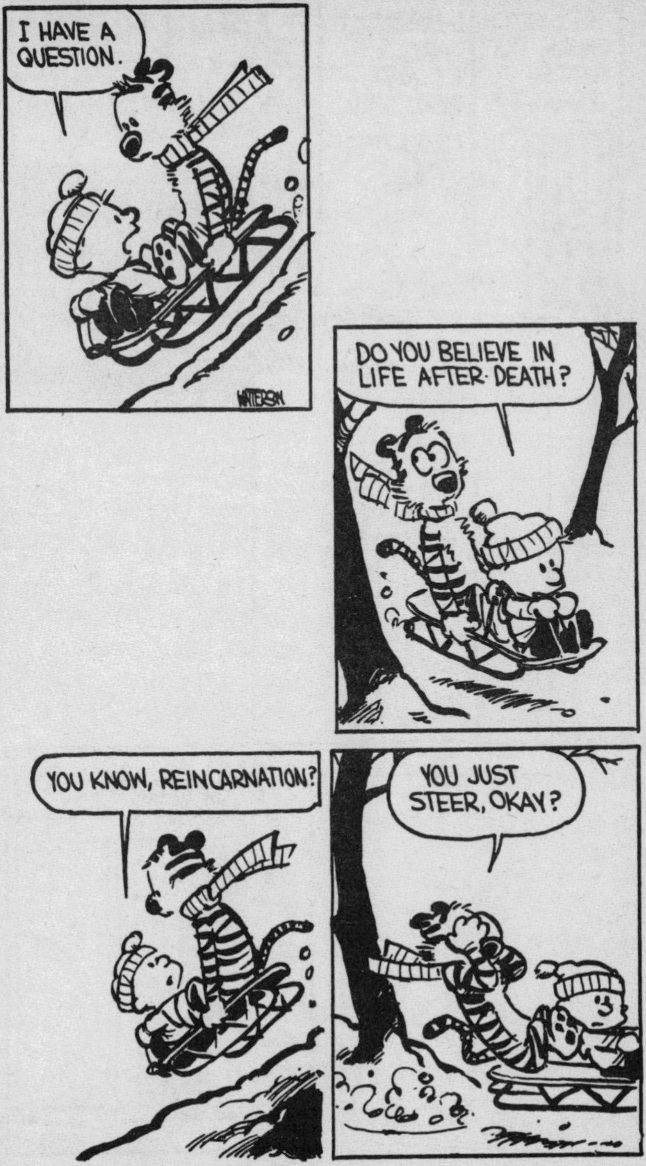
I HAVE A QUESTION.
WATTERSON
DO YOU BELIEVE IN LIFE AFTER DEATH?
YOU KNOW, REINCARNATION?
YOU JUST STEER, OKAY?

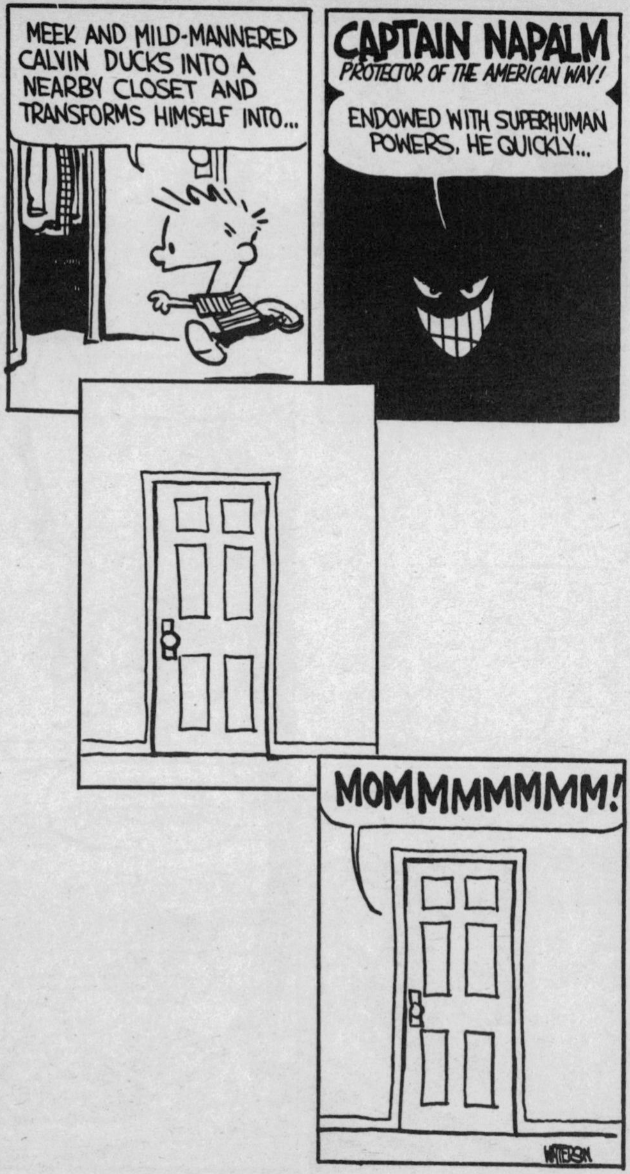
MEEK AND MILD-MANNERED CALVIN DUCKS INTO A NEARBY CLOSET AND TRANSFORMS HIMSELF INTO...
CAPTAIN NAPALM
PROTECTOR OF THE AMERICAN WAY!
ENDOWED WITH SUPERHUMAN POWERS, HE QUICKLY...
MOMMMMMMM!
WATERSON

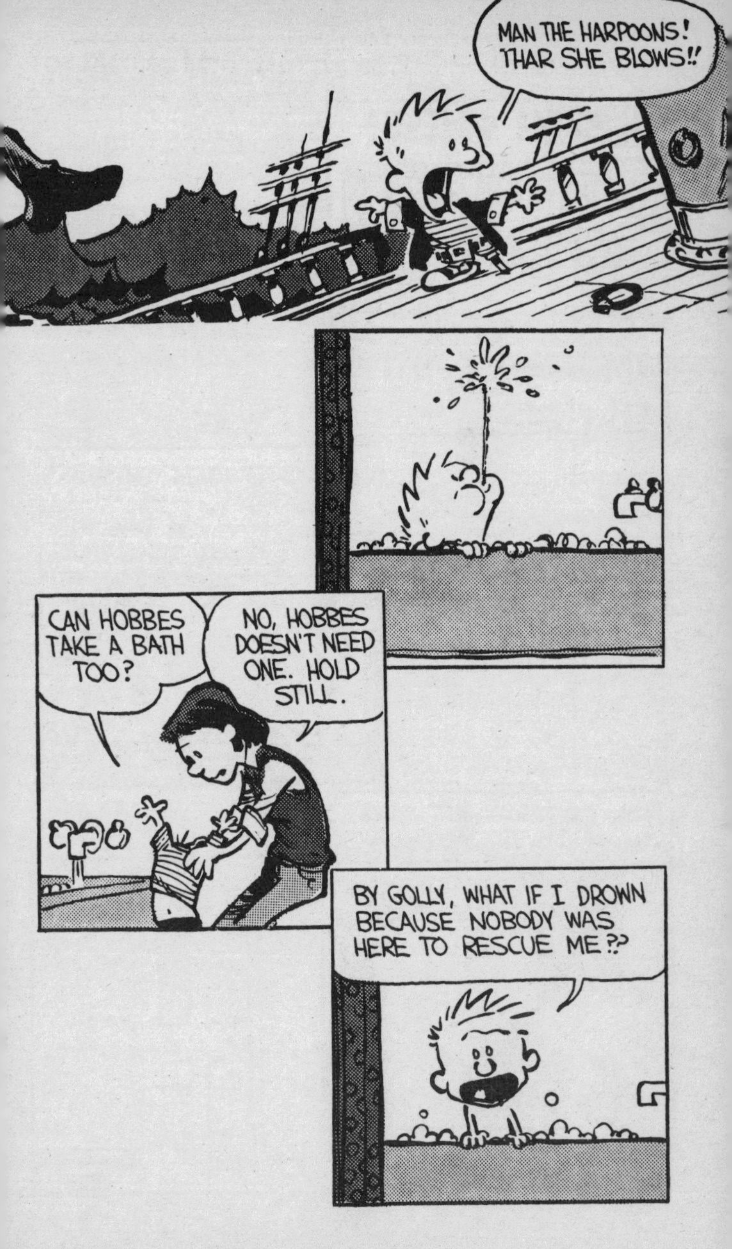
MAN THE HARPOONS! THAR SHE BLOWS!!
CAN HOBBES TAKE A BATH TOO?
NO, HOBBES DOESN'T NEED ONE. HOLD STILL.
BY GOLLY, WHAT IF I DROWN BECAUSE NOBODY WAS HERE TO RESCUE ME??

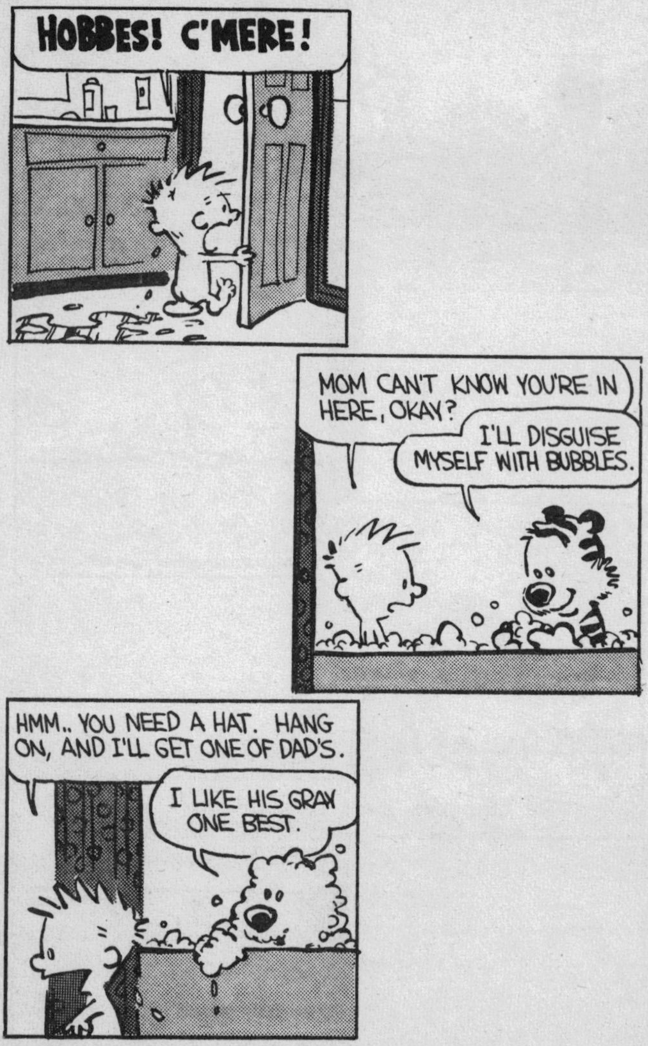
HOBBES! C'MERE!
MOM CAN'T KNOW YOU'RE IN HERE, OKAY?
I'LL DISGUISE MYSELF WITH BUBBLES.
HMM.. YOU NEED A HAT. HANG ON, AND I'LL GET ONE OF DAD'S.
I LIKE HIS GRAY ONE BEST.

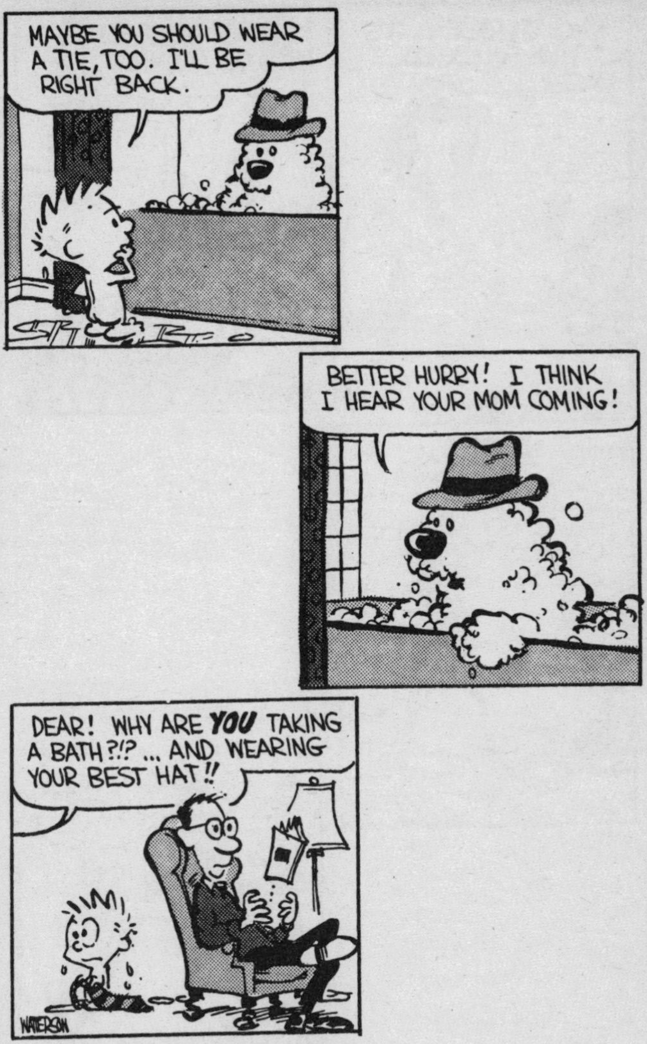
MAYBE YOU SHOULD WEAR A TIE, TOO. I'LL BE RIGHT BACK.
BETTER HURRY! I THINK I HEAR YOUR MOM COMING!
DEAR! WHY ARE **YOU** TAKING A BATH?!? ... AND WEARING YOUR BEST HAT!!
WATERSON

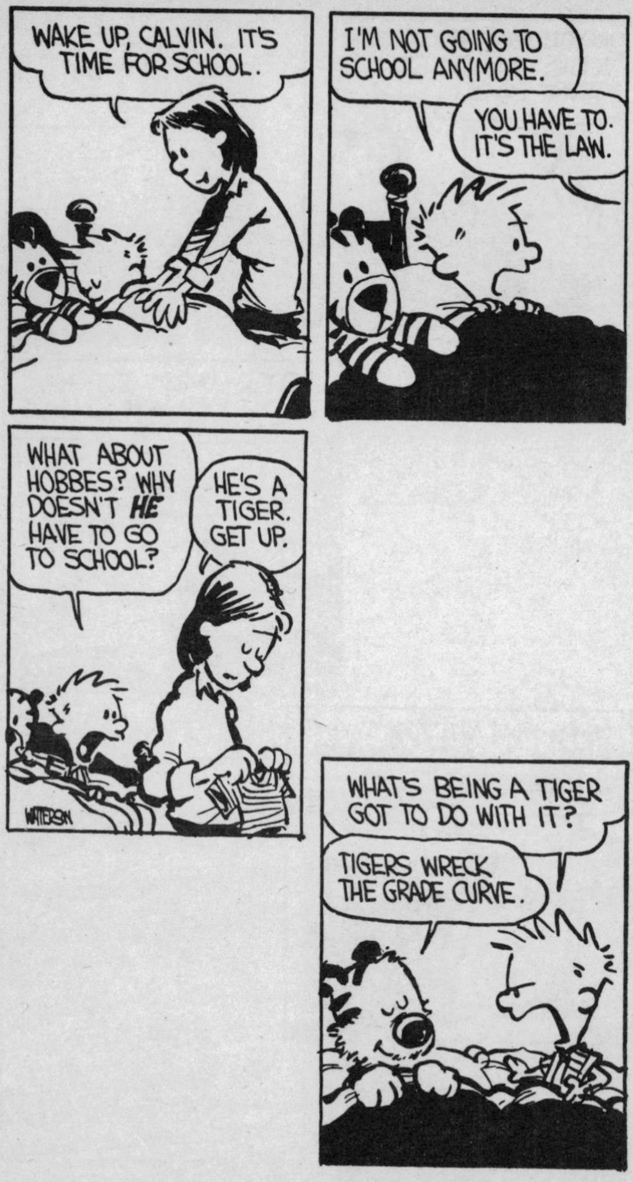

WAKE UP, CALVIN. IT'S TIME FOR SCHOOL.
I'M NOT GOING TO SCHOOL ANYMORE.
YOU HAVE TO. IT'S THE LAW.
WHAT ABOUT HOBBES? WHY DOESN'T *HE* HAVE TO GO TO SCHOOL?
HE'S A TIGER. GET UP.
WATTERSON
WHAT'S BEING A TIGER GOT TO DO WITH IT?
TIGERS WRECK THE GRADE CURVE.

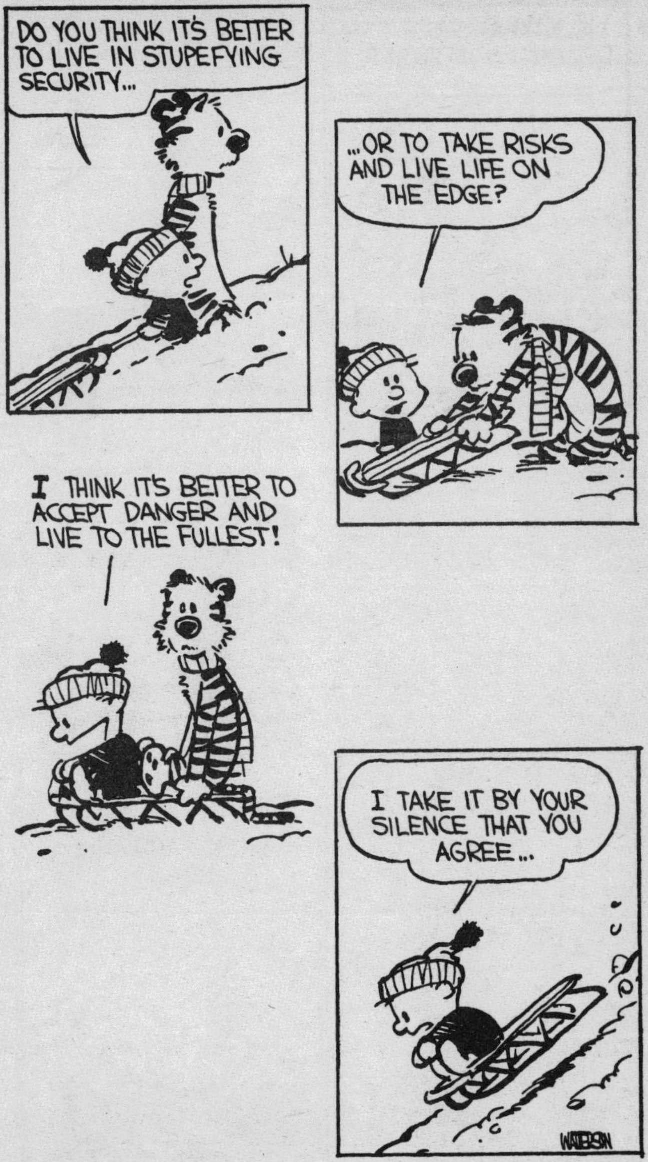
DO YOU THINK IT'S BETTER TO LIVE IN STUPEFYING SECURITY...
...OR TO TAKE RISKS AND LIVE LIFE ON THE EDGE?
I THINK IT'S BETTER TO ACCEPT DANGER AND LIVE TO THE FULLEST!
I TAKE IT BY YOUR SILENCE THAT YOU AGREE...
WATTERSON

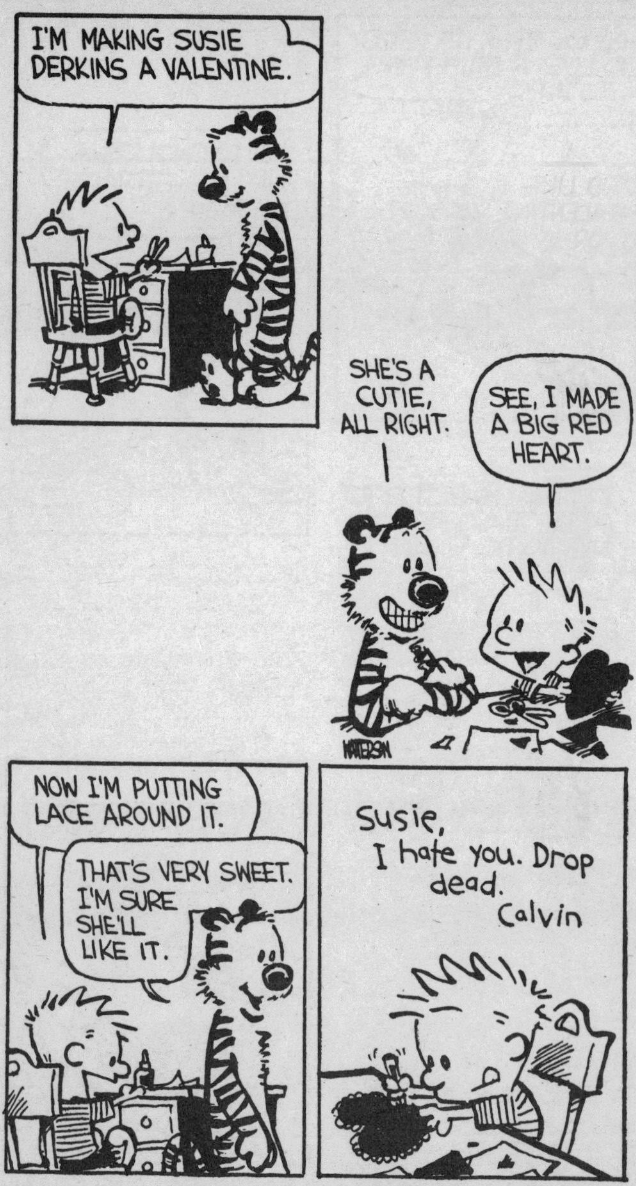

I'M MAKING SUSIE DERKINS A VALENTINE.
SHE'S A CUTIE, ALL RIGHT.
SEE, I MADE A BIG RED HEART.
WATTERSON
NOW I'M PUTTING LACE AROUND IT.
THAT'S VERY SWEET. I'M SURE SHE'LL LIKE IT.
Susie,
I hate you. Drop dead.
Calvin

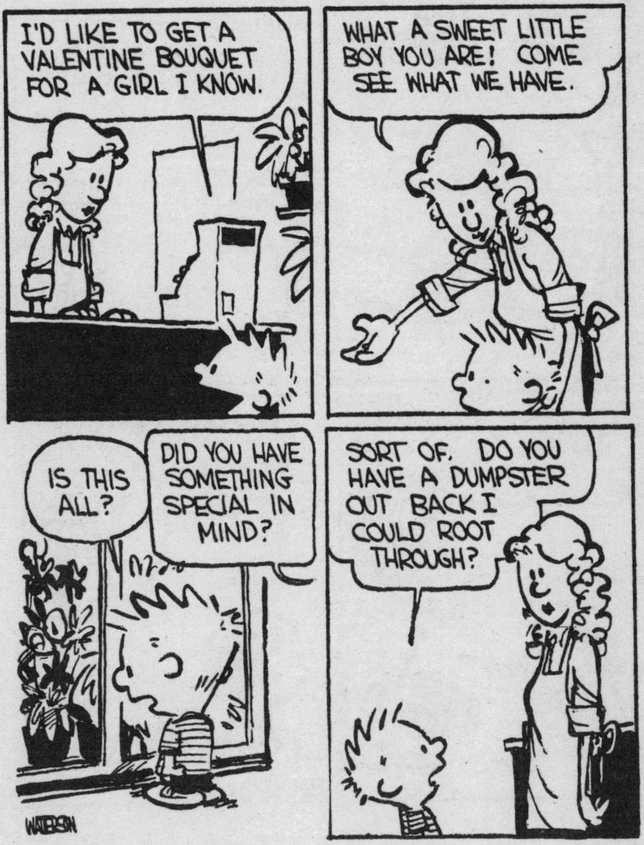
I'D LIKE TO GET A VALENTINE BOUQUET FOR A GIRL I KNOW.
WHAT A SWEET LITTLE BOY YOU ARE! COME SEE WHAT WE HAVE.
IS THIS ALL?
DID YOU HAVE SOMETHING SPECIAL IN MIND?
SORT OF. DO YOU HAVE A DUMPSTER OUT BACK I COULD ROOT THROUGH?
WATTERSON

CALVIN, YOU BALONEY BRAIN!
!
YOU SENT ME A HATE-MAIL VALENTINE AND A CRUMMY BUNCH OF DEAD FLOWERS!
SO HERE'S A VALENTINE FOR *YOU*, YOU INSENSITIVE CLOD!!
POW
A VALENTINE AND FLOWERS! HE *LIKES* ME!
SHE NOTICED! SHE *LIKES* ME!
WATTERSON

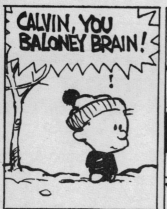

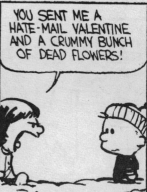

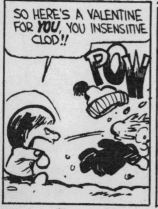

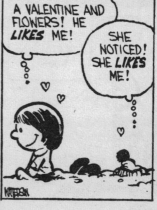

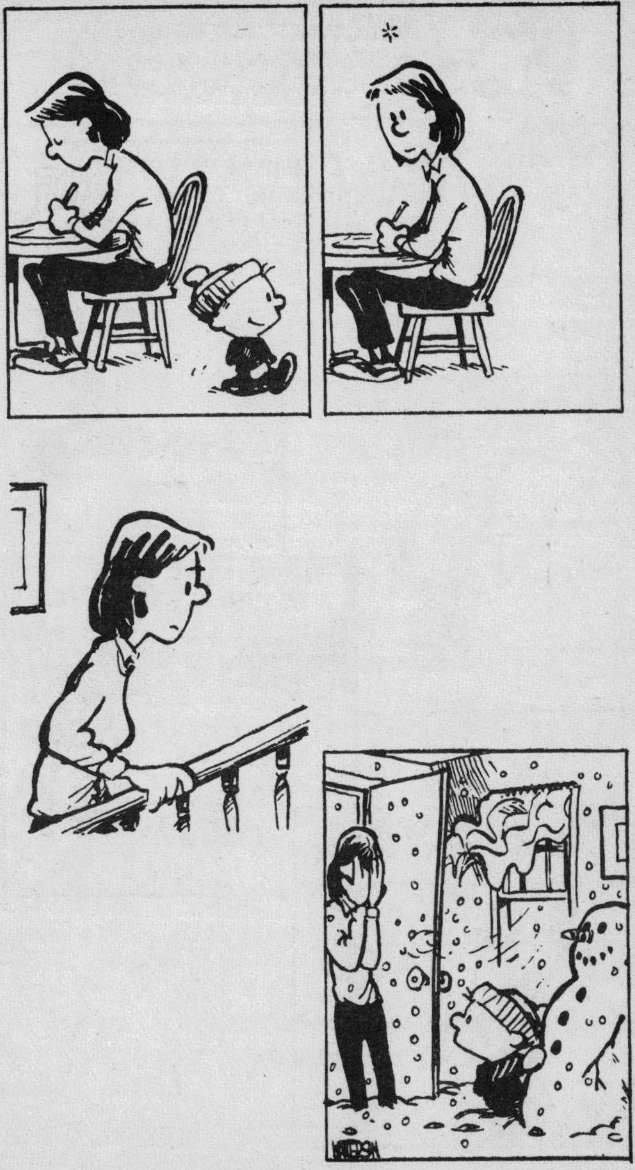

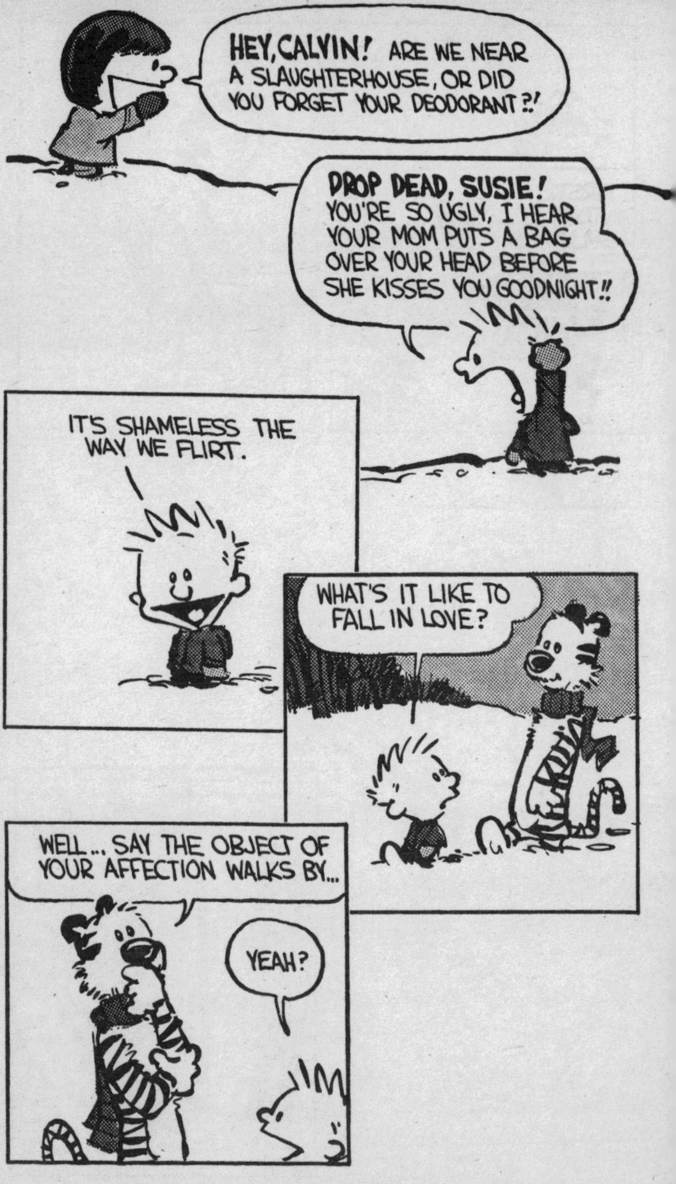
HEY, CALVIN! ARE WE NEAR A SLAUGHTERHOUSE, OR DID YOU FORGET YOUR DEODORANT?!
DROP DEAD, SUSIE! YOU'RE SO UGLY, I HEAR YOUR MOM PUTS A BAG OVER YOUR HEAD BEFORE SHE KISSES YOU GOODNIGHT!!
IT'S SHAMELESS THE WAY WE FLIRT.
WHAT'S IT LIKE TO FALL IN LOVE?
WELL... SAY THE OBJECT OF YOUR AFFECTION WALKS BY...
YEAH?

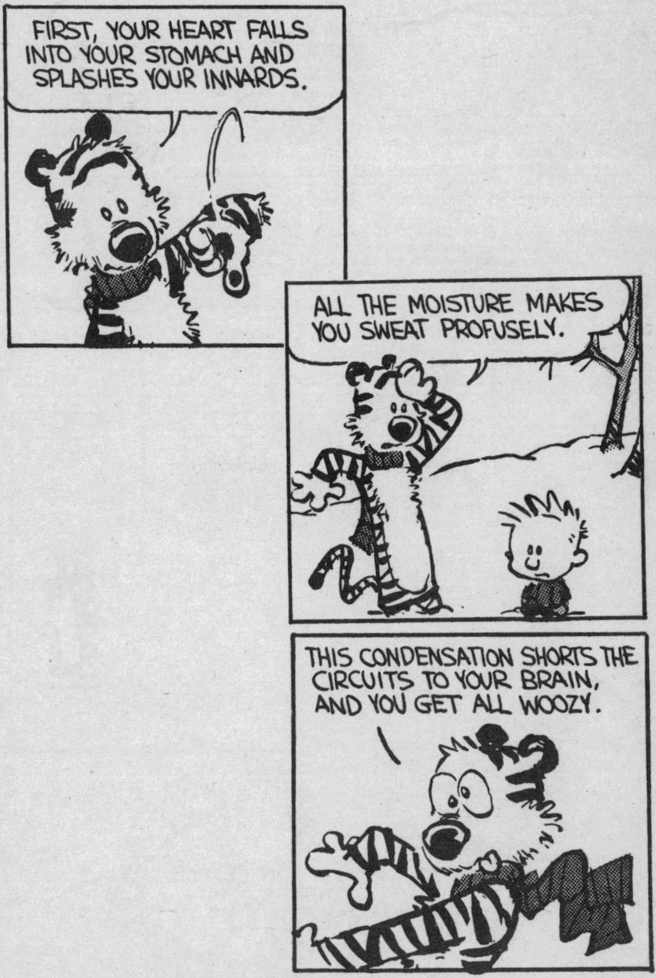
FIRST, YOUR HEART FALLS INTO YOUR STOMACH AND SPLASHES YOUR INNARDS.
ALL THE MOISTURE MAKES YOU SWEAT PROFUSELY.
THIS CONDENSATION SHORTS THE CIRCUITS TO YOUR BRAIN, AND YOU GET ALL WOOZY.

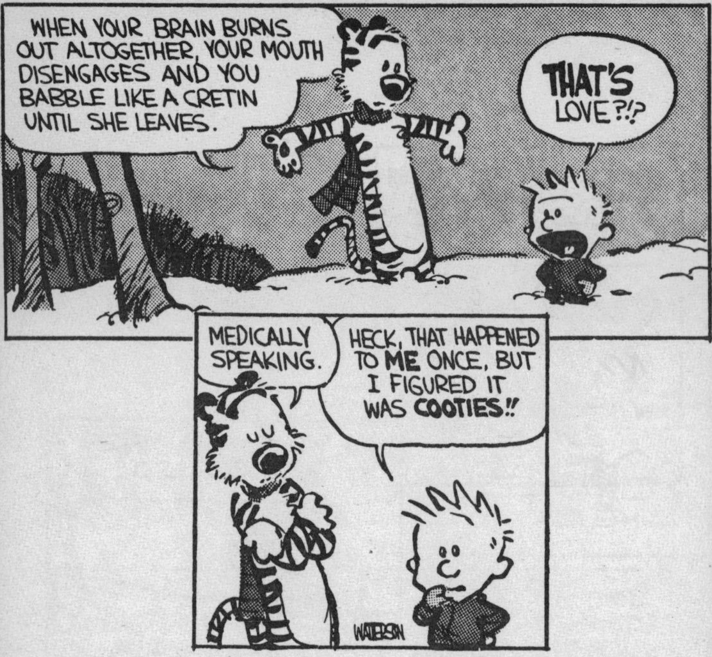
WHEN YOUR BRAIN BURNS OUT ALTOGETHER, YOUR MOUTH DISENGAGES AND YOU BABBLE LIKE A CRETIN UNTIL SHE LEAVES.
THAT'S LOVE?!?
MEDICALLY SPEAKING.
HECK, THAT HAPPENED TO ME ONCE, BUT I FIGURED IT WAS COOTIES!!
WATTERSON

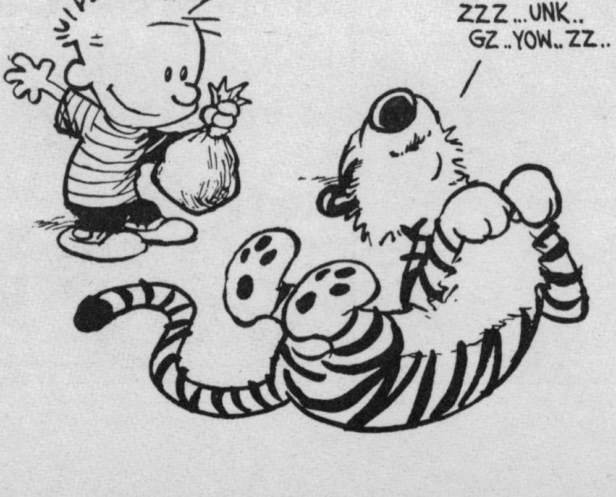
ZZZ...UNK.. GZ..YOW..ZZ..

Hey, Calvin, it's gonna cost you 50 cents to be my friend today.
AND WHAT IF I DON'T *WANT* TO BE YOUR FRIEND TODAY?
Then the janitor scrapes you off the wall with a spatula.
HECK, WHAT'S A LITTLE EXTORTION AMONG FRIENDS?
WATTERSON

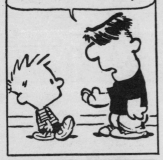

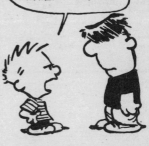

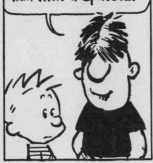

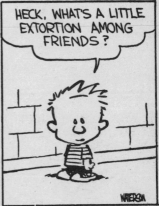

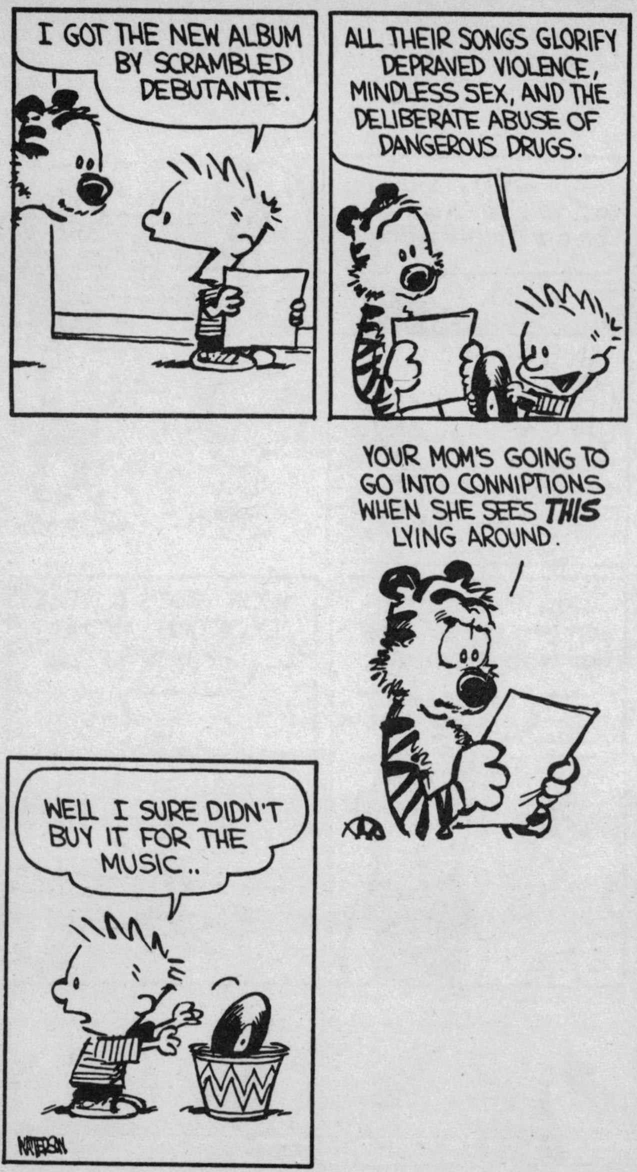
I GOT THE NEW ALBUM BY SCRAMBLED DEBUTANTE.
ALL THEIR SONGS GLORIFY DEPRAVED VIOLENCE, MINDLESS SEX, AND THE DELIBERATE ABUSE OF DANGEROUS DRUGS.
YOUR MOM'S GOING TO GO INTO CONNIPTIONS WHEN SHE SEES ***THIS*** LYING AROUND.
WELL I SURE DIDN'T BUY IT FOR THE MUSIC..
WATTERSON

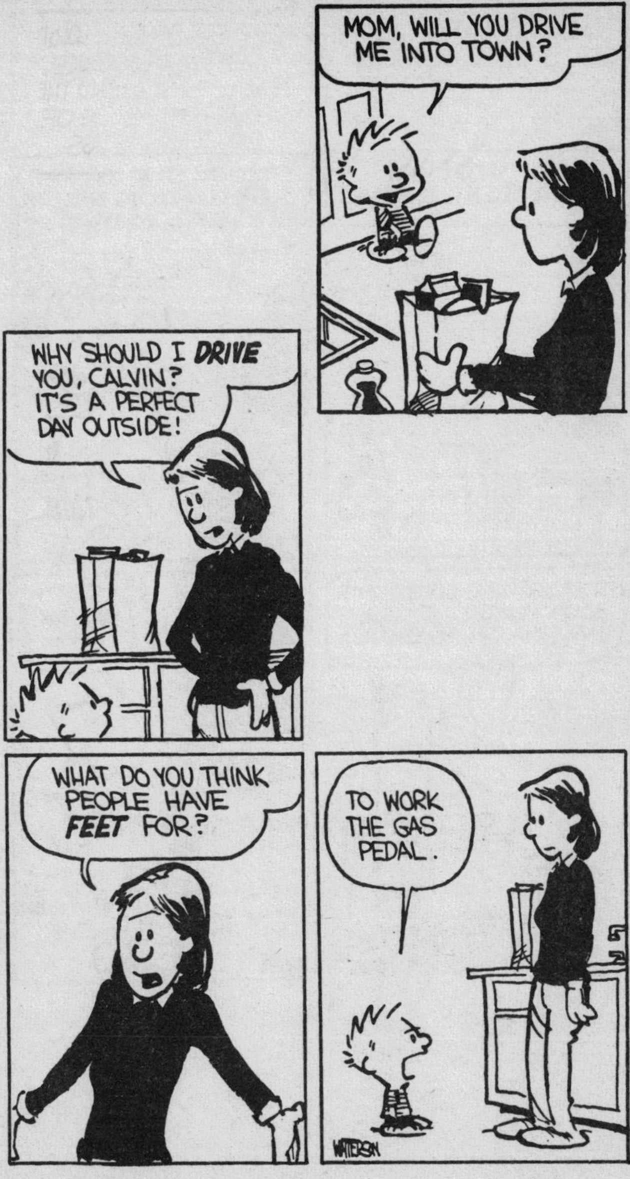
MOM, WILL YOU DRIVE ME INTO TOWN?
WHY SHOULD I **DRIVE** YOU, CALVIN? IT'S A PERFECT DAY OUTSIDE!
WHAT DO YOU THINK PEOPLE HAVE **FEET** FOR?
TO WORK THE GAS PEDAL.
WATTERSON

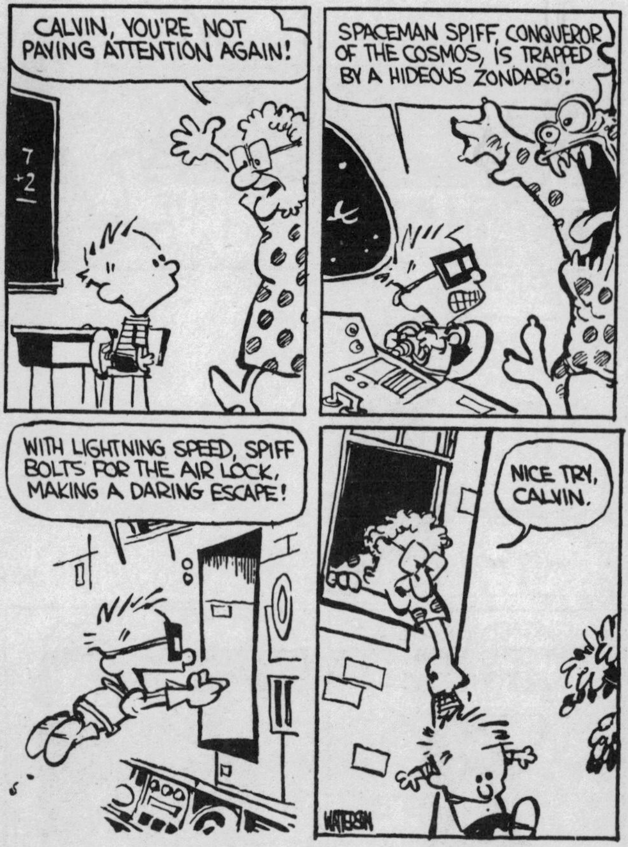
CALVIN, YOU'RE NOT PAYING ATTENTION AGAIN!
SPACEMAN SPIFF, CONQUEROR OF THE COSMOS, IS TRAPPED BY A HIDEOUS ZONDARG!
WITH LIGHTNING SPEED, SPIFF BOLTS FOR THE AIR LOCK, MAKING A DARING ESCAPE!
NICE TRY, CALVIN.
WATERSON

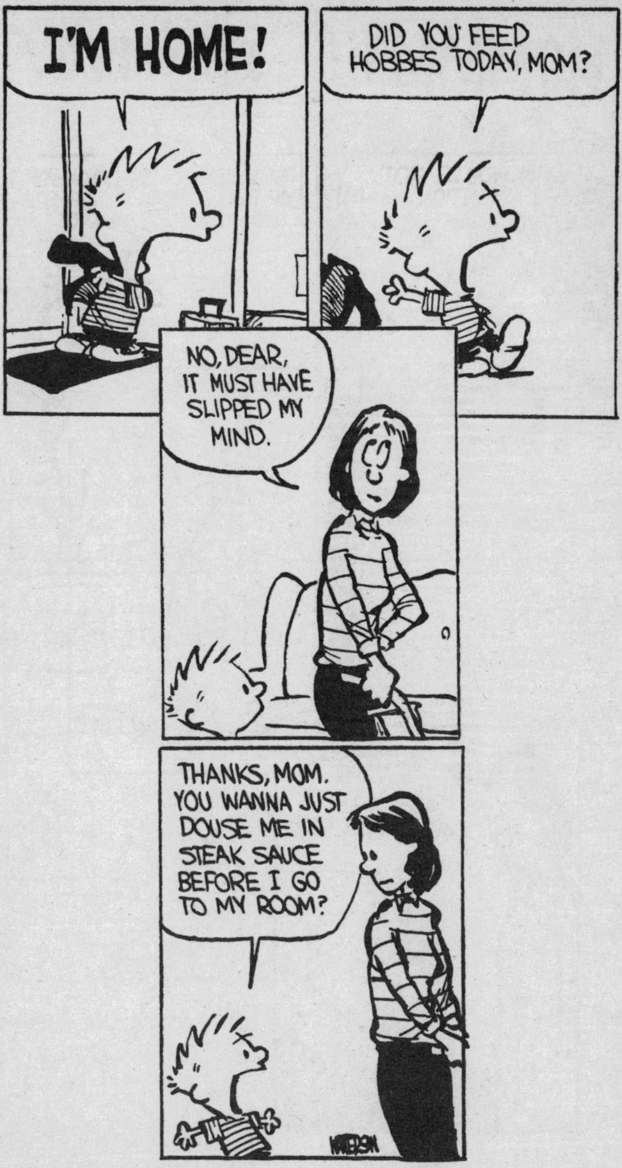
I'M HOME!
DID YOU FEED HOBBES TODAY, MOM?
NO, DEAR, IT MUST HAVE SLIPPED MY MIND.
THANKS, MOM. YOU WANNA JUST DOUSE ME IN STEAK SAUCE BEFORE I GO TO MY ROOM?
WATTERSON

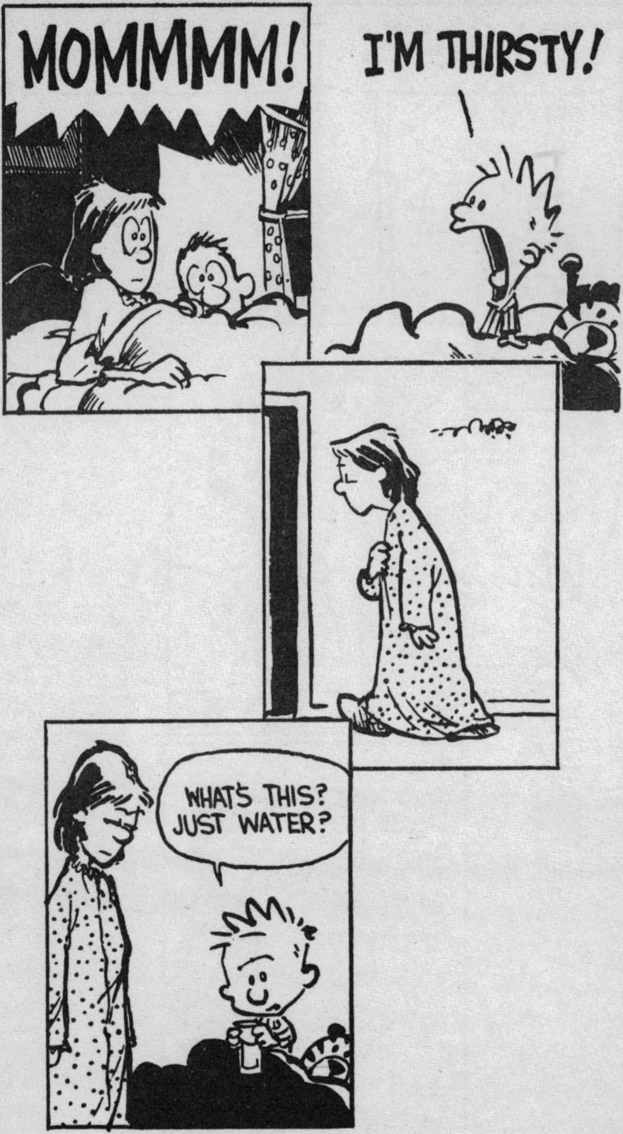
MOMMMM!
I'M THIRSTY!
WHAT'S THIS? JUST WATER?

Finis

Time Warner Paperback titles available by post:

☐ Calvin and Hobbes Vol. 2	Bill Watterson	£4.99
☐ Calvin and Hobbes Vol. 3	Bill Watterson	£4.99
☐ Something Under the Bed is Drooling	Bill Watterson	£7.99
☐ Yukon Ho!	Bill Watterson	£7.99
☐ Weirdos From Another Planet	Bill Watterson	£7.99
☐ Lazy Sunday Book	Bill Watterson	£9.99
☐ Revenge of the Baby-Sat	Bill Watterson	£7.99
☐ Authoritative Calvin and Hobbes	Bill Watterson	£10.99
☐ Scientific Progress Goes 'Boink'	Bill Watterson	£7.99
☐ Attack of the Deranged Mutant Killer Monster Snow Goons	Bill Watterson	£7.99
☐ The Days Are Just Packed	Bill Watterson	£10.99
☐ Homicidal Psycho Jungle Cat	Bill Watterson	£10.99

The prices shown above are correct at time of going to press. However, the publishers reserve the right to increase prices on covers from those previously advertised without prior notice.

timewarner
paperbacks

TIME WARNER PAPERBACKS
P.O. Box 121, Kettering, Northants NN14 4ZQ
Tel: 01832 737525, Fax: 01832 733076
Email: aspenhouse@FSBDial.co.uk

POST AND PACKING:
Payments can be made as follows: cheque, postal order (payable to Time Warner Books) or by credit cards. Do not send cash or currency.

All U.K. Orders	**FREE OF CHARGE**
E.E.C. & Overseas	25% of order value

Name (Block Letters) _____

Address_____

_____

Post/zip code:_____

☐ Please keep me in touch with future Time Warner publications

☐ I enclose my remittance £_____

☐ I wish to pay by Visa/Access/Mastercard/Eurocard

Card Expiry Date

_____